THE COMIC COLLECTION

A GERRY ANDERSON PRODUCTION

THUNDERBIRDS ™

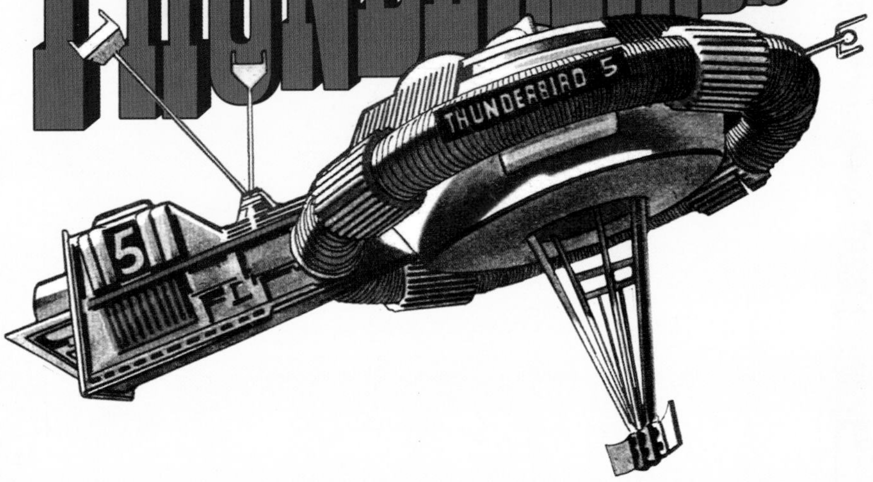

CLASSIC COMICS

EGMONT

EGMONT

This volume first published in Great Britain 2014 by Egmont UK Limited
The Yellow Building, 1 Nicholas Road, London W11 4AN
Thunderbirds ™ and © ITC Entertainment Group Limited 1964, 1999 and 2014.
Licensed by ITV Ventures Limited. All rights reserved.

A GERRY ANDERSON PRODUCTION

Cover illustration by Steve Kyte

ISBN 978 1 4052 7264 3
57361/1
Printed in Malaysia.

Please note: Some of the comic strips used in this collection
are exceedingly rare, so the print quality may vary.

MIX
Paper from
responsible sources
FSC® C018306

Egmont is passionate about helping to preserve the world's remaining ancient forests.
We only use paper from legal and sustainable forest sources.

This book is made from paper certified by the Forest Stewardship Council® (FSC®),
an organisation dedicated to promoting responsible management of forest resources.
For more information on the FSC, please visit www.fsc.org. To learn more about
Egmont's sustainable paper policy, please visit www.egmont.co.uk/ethical

Stay safe online. Egmont is not responsible for content hosted by third parties.

THE COMIC COLLECTION

A GERRY ANDERSON PRODUCTION

THUNDERBIRDS ™

VOLUME FIVE

CLASSIC COMICS

EGMONT

CONTENTS

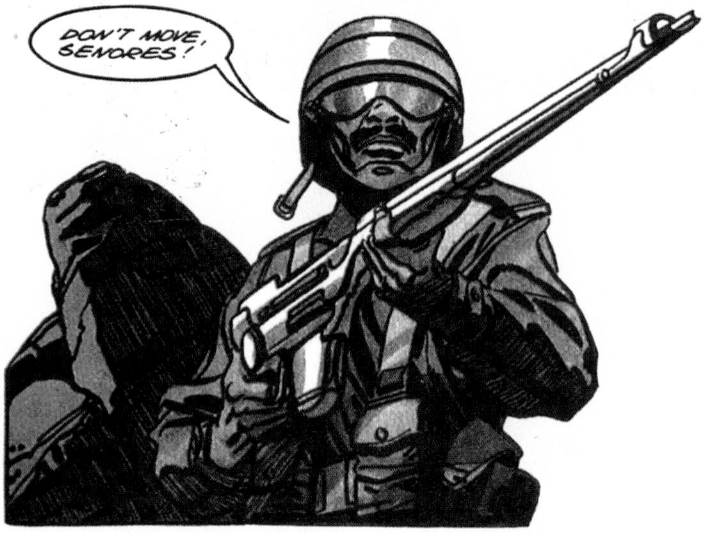

DON'T MOVE, SENORES!

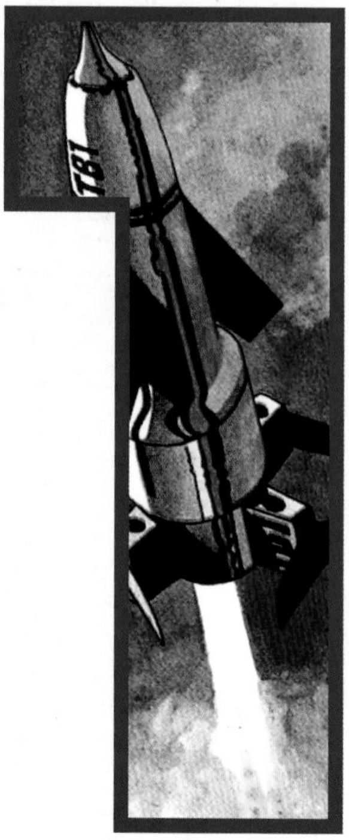

TB1

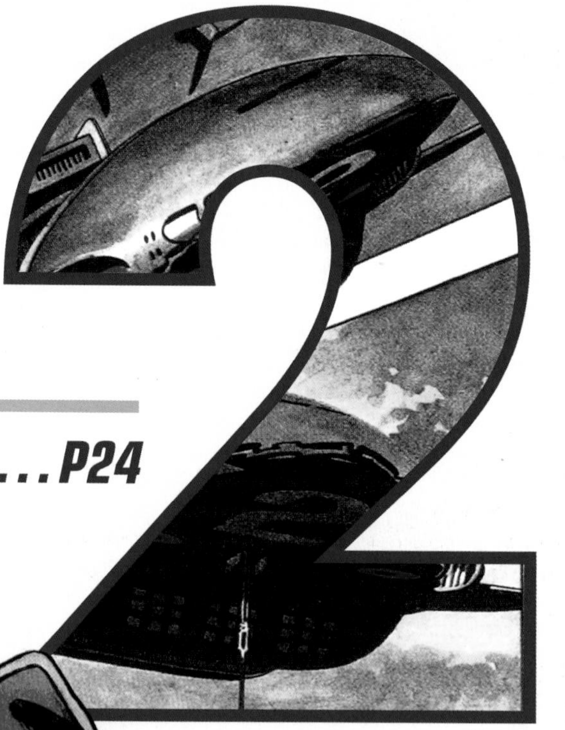

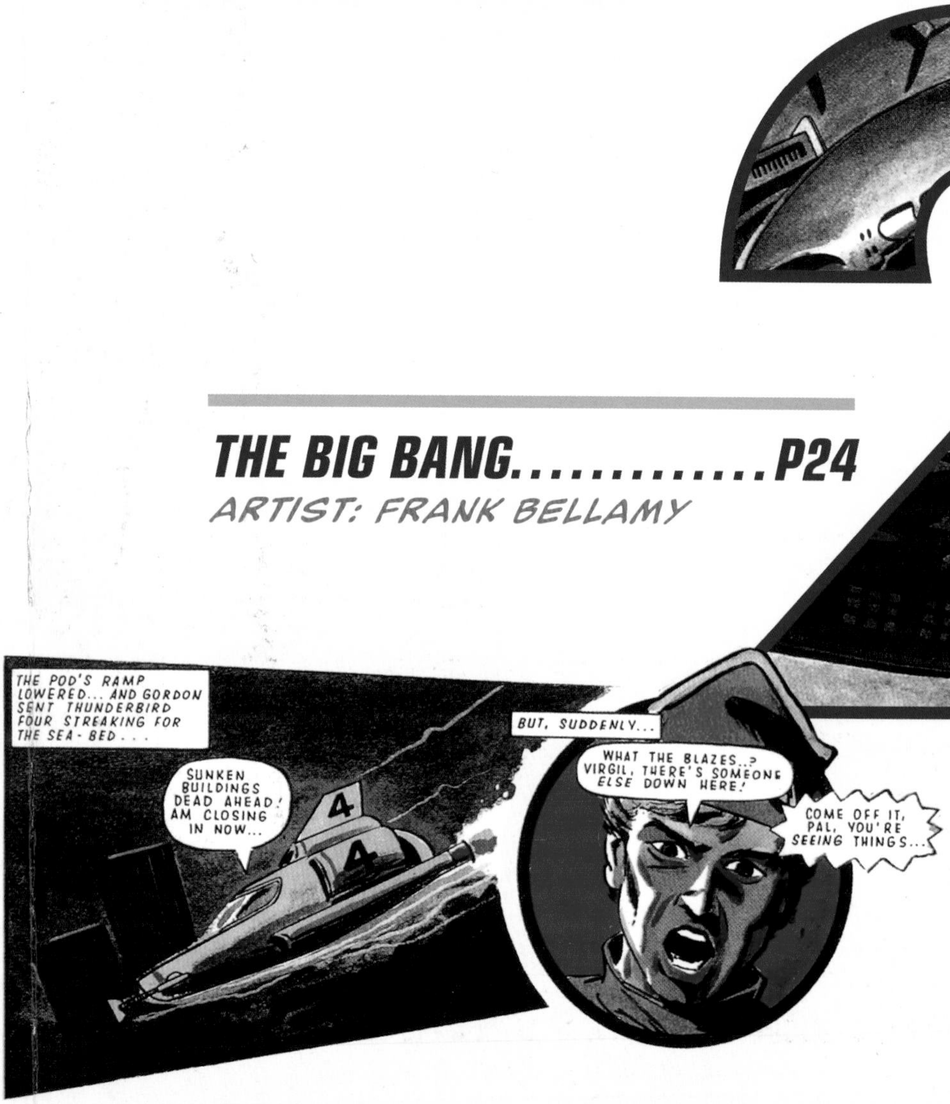

THE POD'S RAMP LOWERED... AND GORDON SENT THUNDERBIRD FOUR STREAKING FOR THE SEA-BED...
SUNKEN BUILDINGS DEAD AHEAD! AM CLOSING IN NOW...
4
BUT, SUDDENLY...
WHAT THE BLAZES..? VIRGIL, THERE'S SOMEONE ELSE DOWN HERE!
COME OFF IT, PAL, YOU'RE SEEING THINGS...

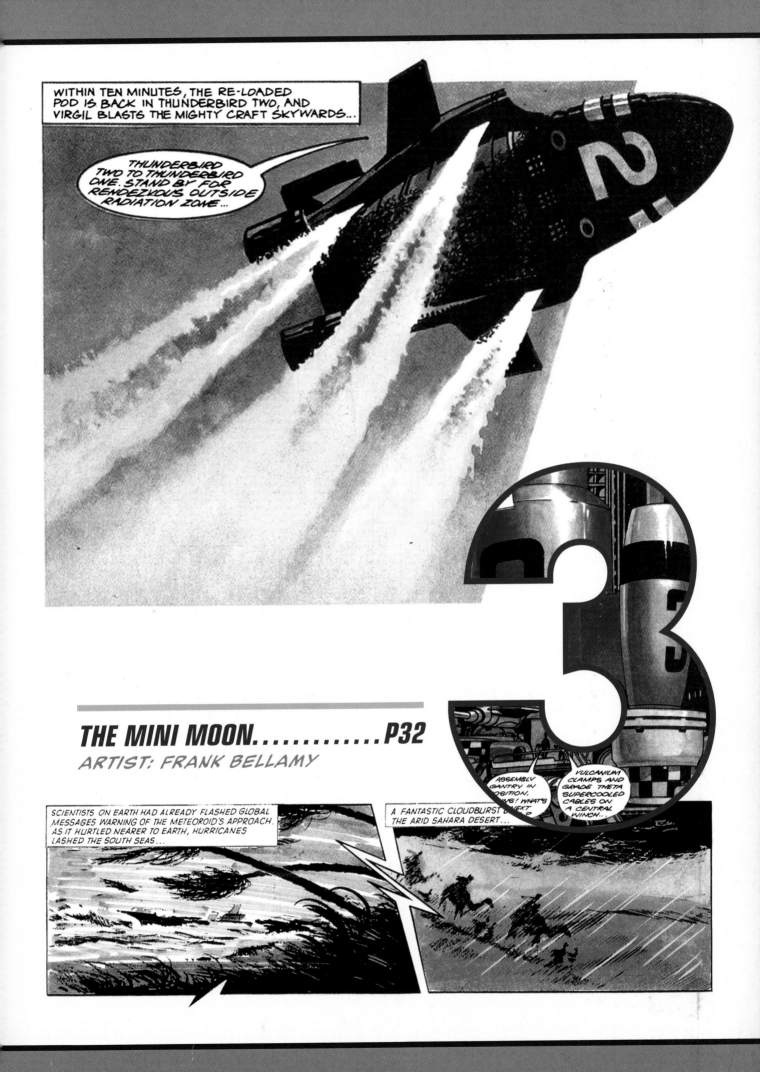

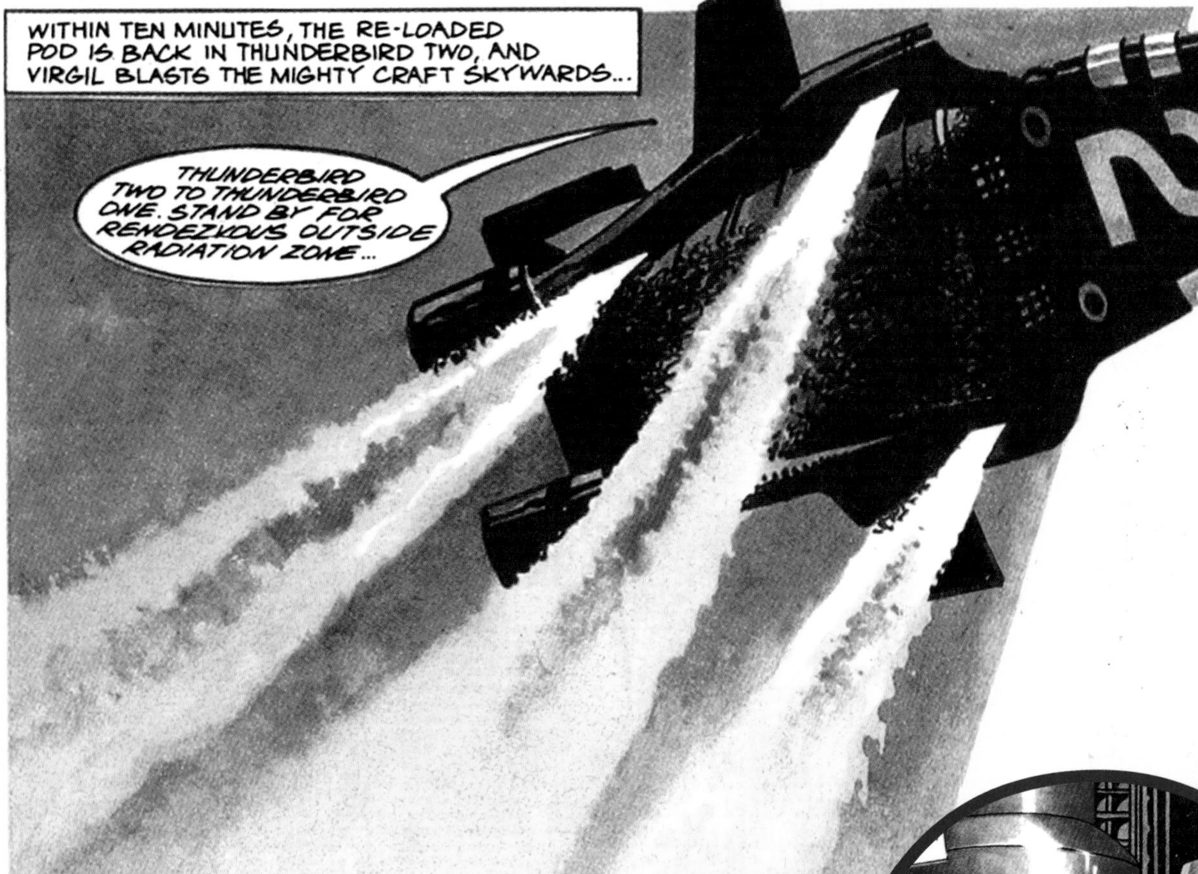
WITHIN TEN MINUTES, THE RE-LOADED POD IS BACK IN THUNDERBIRD TWO, AND VIRGIL BLASTS THE MIGHTY CRAFT SKYWARDS...
THUNDERBIRD TWO TO THUNDERBIRD ONE. STAND BY FOR RENDEZVOUS OUTSIDE RADIATION ZONE...

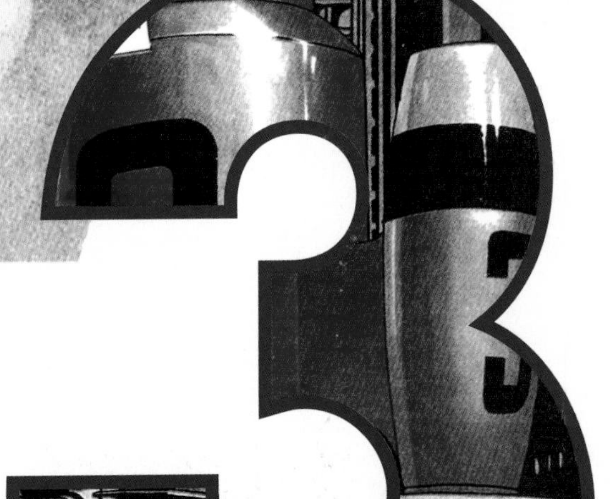
VULCANIUM CLAMPS AND GRADE THETA SUPERCOOLED CABLES ON A CENTRAL WINCH...

THE MINI MOON..............P32

ARTIST: FRANK BELLAMY

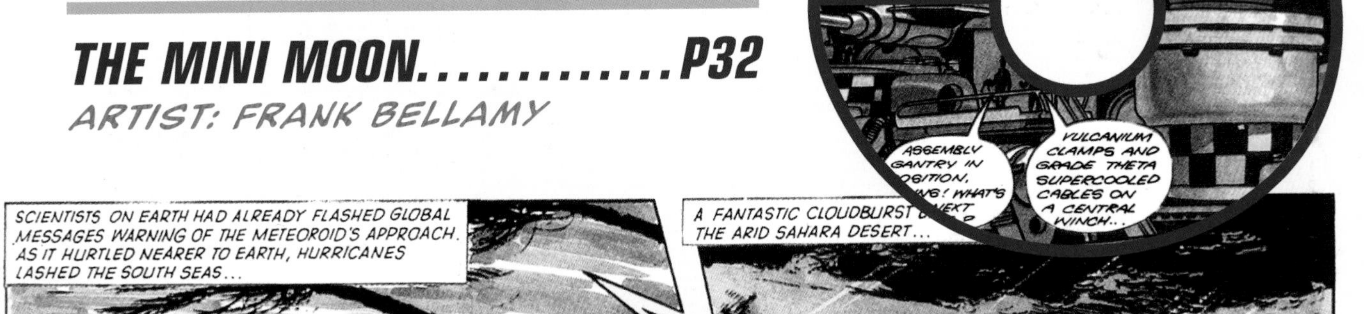
SCIENTISTS ON EARTH HAD ALREADY FLASHED GLOBAL MESSAGES WARNING OF THE METEOROID'S APPROACH. AS IT HURTLED NEARER TO EARTH, HURRICANES LASHED THE SOUTH SEAS...
A FANTASTIC CLOUDBURST
THE ARID SAHARA DESERT...

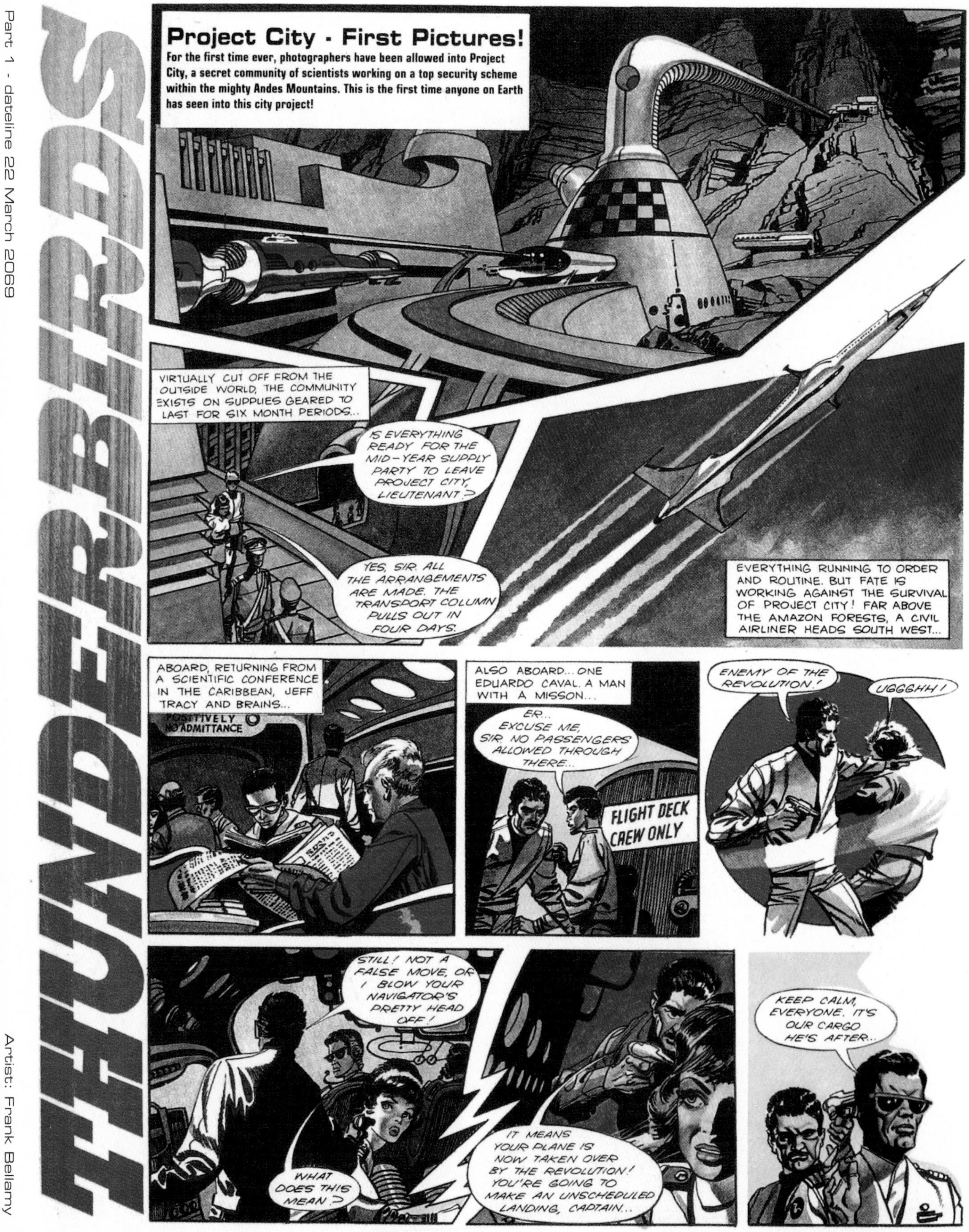
THUNDERBIRDS
Part 1 - dateline 22 March 2069
Artist: Frank Bellamy
Project City - First Pictures!
For the first time ever, photographers have been allowed into Project City, a secret community of scientists working on a top security scheme within the mighty Andes Mountains. This is the first time anyone on Earth has seen into this city project!
VIRTUALLY CUT OFF FROM THE OUTSIDE WORLD, THE COMMUNITY EXISTS ON SUPPLIES GEARED TO LAST FOR SIX MONTH PERIODS...
IS EVERYTHING READY FOR THE MID-YEAR SUPPLY PARTY TO LEAVE PROJECT CITY, LIEUTENANT?
YES, SIR. ALL THE ARRANGEMENTS ARE MADE. THE TRANSPORT COLUMN PULLS OUT IN FOUR DAYS.
EVERYTHING RUNNING TO ORDER AND ROUTINE. BUT FATE IS WORKING AGAINST THE SURVIVAL OF PROJECT CITY! FAR ABOVE THE AMAZON FORESTS, A CIVIL AIRLINER HEADS SOUTH WEST...
ABOARD, RETURNING FROM A SCIENTIFIC CONFERENCE IN THE CARIBBEAN, JEFF TRACY AND BRAINS...
POSITIVELY NO ADMITTANCE
ALSO ABOARD... ONE EDUARDO CAVAL. A MAN WITH A MISSON...
ER... EXCUSE ME, SIR. NO PASSENGERS ALLOWED THROUGH THERE...
FLIGHT DECK CREW ONLY
ENEMY OF THE REVOLUTION!
UGGGHH!
STILL! NOT A FALSE MOVE, OR I BLOW YOUR NAVIGATOR'S PRETTY HEAD OFF!
WHAT DOES THIS MEAN?
IT MEANS YOUR PLANE IS NOW TAKEN OVER BY THE REVOLUTION! YOU'RE GOING TO MAKE AN UNSCHEDULED LANDING, CAPTAIN...
KEEP CALM, EVERYONE. IT'S OUR CARGO HE'S AFTER...

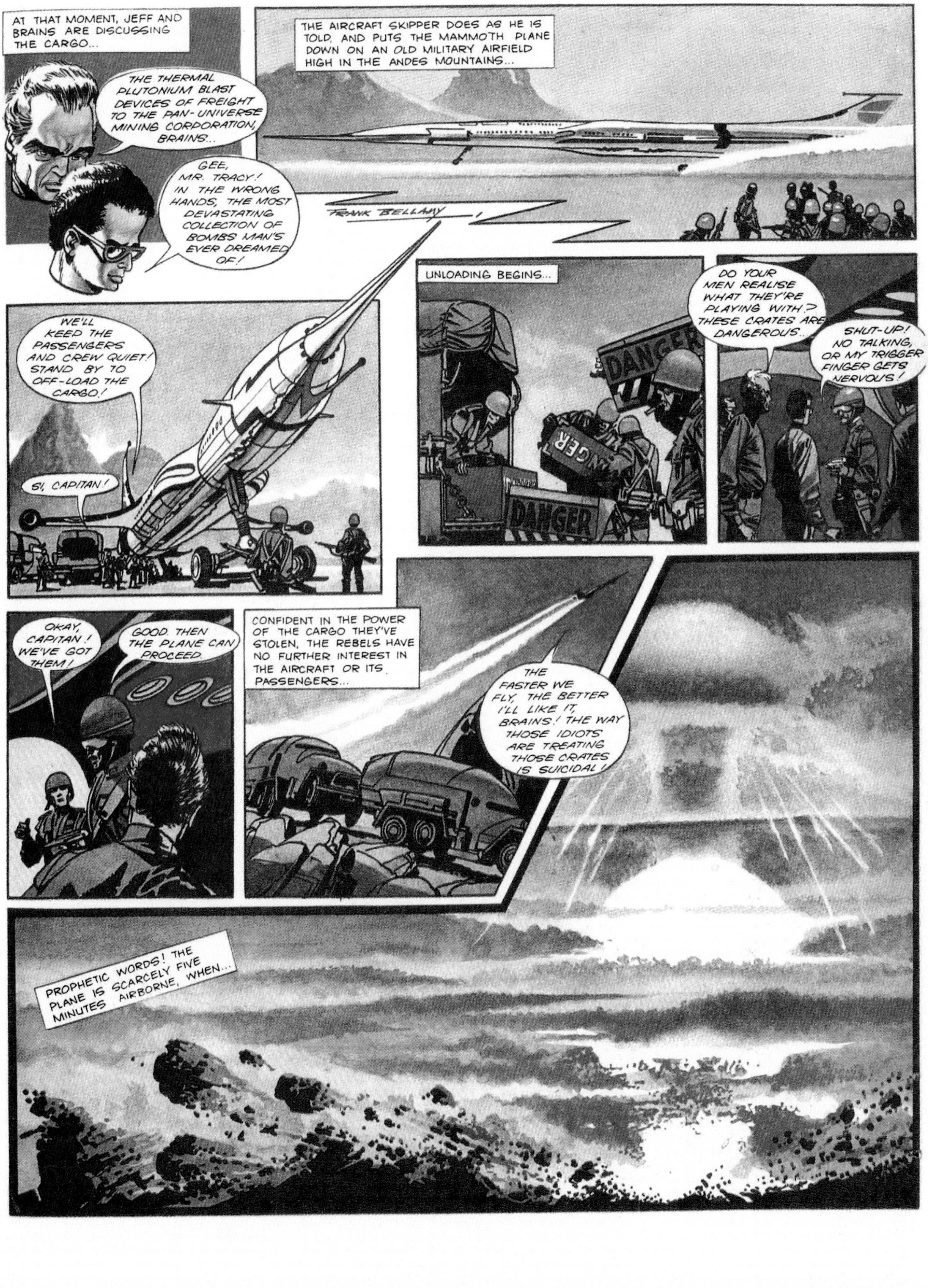
AT THAT MOMENT, JEFF AND BRAINS ARE DISCUSSING THE CARGO...
THE THERMAL PLUTONIUM BLAST DEVICES OF FREIGHT TO THE PAN-UNIVERSE MINING CORPORATION, BRAINS...
GEE, MR. TRACY! IN THE WRONG HANDS, THE MOST DEVASTATING COLLECTION OF BOMBS MAN'S EVER DREAMED OF!
THE AIRCRAFT SKIPPER DOES AS HE IS TOLD, AND PUTS THE MAMMOTH PLANE DOWN ON AN OLD MILITARY AIRFIELD HIGH IN THE ANDES MOUNTAINS...
FRANK BELLAMY
WE'LL KEEP THE PASSENGERS AND CREW QUIET! STAND BY TO OFF-LOAD THE CARGO!
SI, CAPITAN!
UNLOADING BEGINS...
DANGER
DANGER
DANGER
DO YOUR MEN REALISE WHAT THEY'RE PLAYING WITH? THESE CRATES ARE DANGEROUS...
SHUT-UP! NO TALKING, OR MY TRIGGER FINGER GETS NERVOUS!
OKAY, CAPITAN! WE'VE GOT THEM!
GOOD. THEN THE PLANE CAN PROCEED.
CONFIDENT IN THE POWER OF THE CARGO THEY'VE STOLEN, THE REBELS HAVE NO FURTHER INTEREST IN THE AIRCRAFT OR ITS PASSENGERS...
THE FASTER WE FLY, THE BETTER I'LL LIKE IT, BRAINS! THE WAY THOSE IDIOTS ARE TREATING THOSE CRATES IS SUICIDAL!
PROPHETIC WORDS! THE PLANE IS SCARCELY FIVE MINUTES AIRBORNE, WHEN...

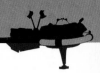

Part 2 - dateline 29 March 2069

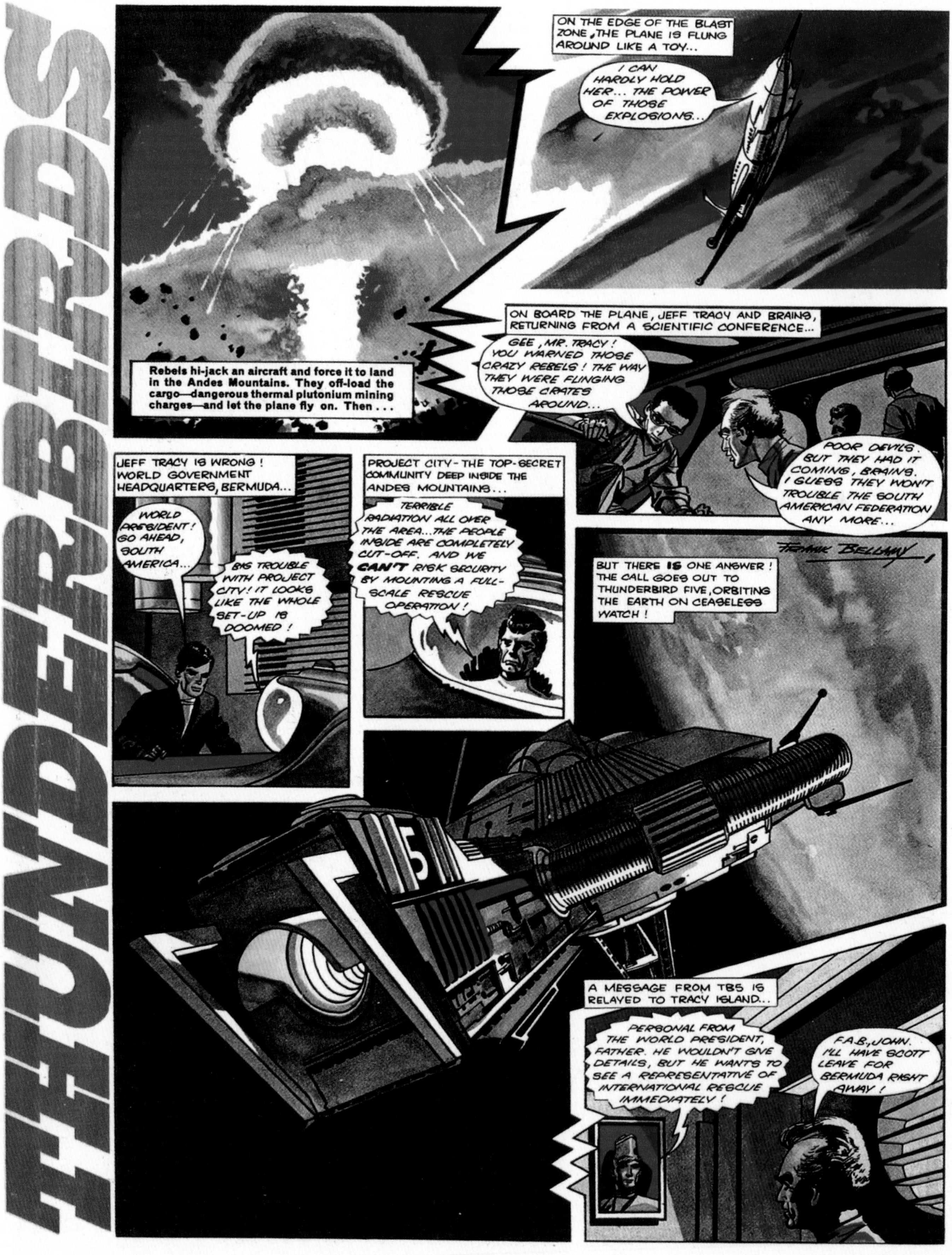
THUNDERBIRDS
Rebels hi-jack an aircraft and force it to land in the Andes Mountains. They off-load the cargo—dangerous thermal plutonium mining charges—and let the plane fly on. Then . . .
ON THE EDGE OF THE BLAST ZONE, THE PLANE IS FLUNG AROUND LIKE A TOY...
I CAN HARDLY HOLD HER... THE POWER OF THOSE EXPLOSIONS...
ON BOARD THE PLANE, JEFF TRACY AND BRAINS, RETURNING FROM A SCIENTIFIC CONFERENCE...
GEE, MR. TRACY! YOU WARNED THOSE CRAZY REBELS! THE WAY THEY WERE FLINGING THOSE CRATES AROUND...
POOR DEVILS. BUT THEY HAD IT COMING, BRAINS. I GUESS THEY WON'T TROUBLE THE SOUTH AMERICAN FEDERATION ANY MORE...
JEFF TRACY IS WRONG! WORLD GOVERNMENT HEADQUARTERS, BERMUDA...
WORLD PRESIDENT! GO AHEAD, SOUTH AMERICA...
BIG TROUBLE WITH PROJECT CITY! IT LOOKS LIKE THE WHOLE SET-UP IS DOOMED!
PROJECT CITY - THE TOP-SECRET COMMUNITY DEEP INSIDE THE ANDES MOUNTAINS...
TERRIBLE RADIATION ALL OVER THE AREA...THE PEOPLE INSIDE ARE COMPLETELY CUT-OFF. AND WE CAN'T RISK SECURITY BY MOUNTING A FULL-SCALE RESCUE OPERATION!
FRANK BELLAMY
BUT THERE IS ONE ANSWER! THE CALL GOES OUT TO THUNDERBIRD FIVE, ORBITING THE EARTH ON CEASELESS WATCH!
5
A MESSAGE FROM TB5 IS RELAYED TO TRACY ISLAND...
PERSONAL FROM THE WORLD PRESIDENT, FATHER. HE WOULDN'T GIVE DETAILS, BUT HE WANTS TO SEE A REPRESENTATIVE OF INTERNATIONAL RESCUE IMMEDIATELY!
F.A.B., JOHN. I'LL HAVE SCOTT LEAVE FOR BERMUDA RIGHT AWAY!

Artist: Frank Bellamy

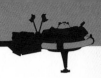

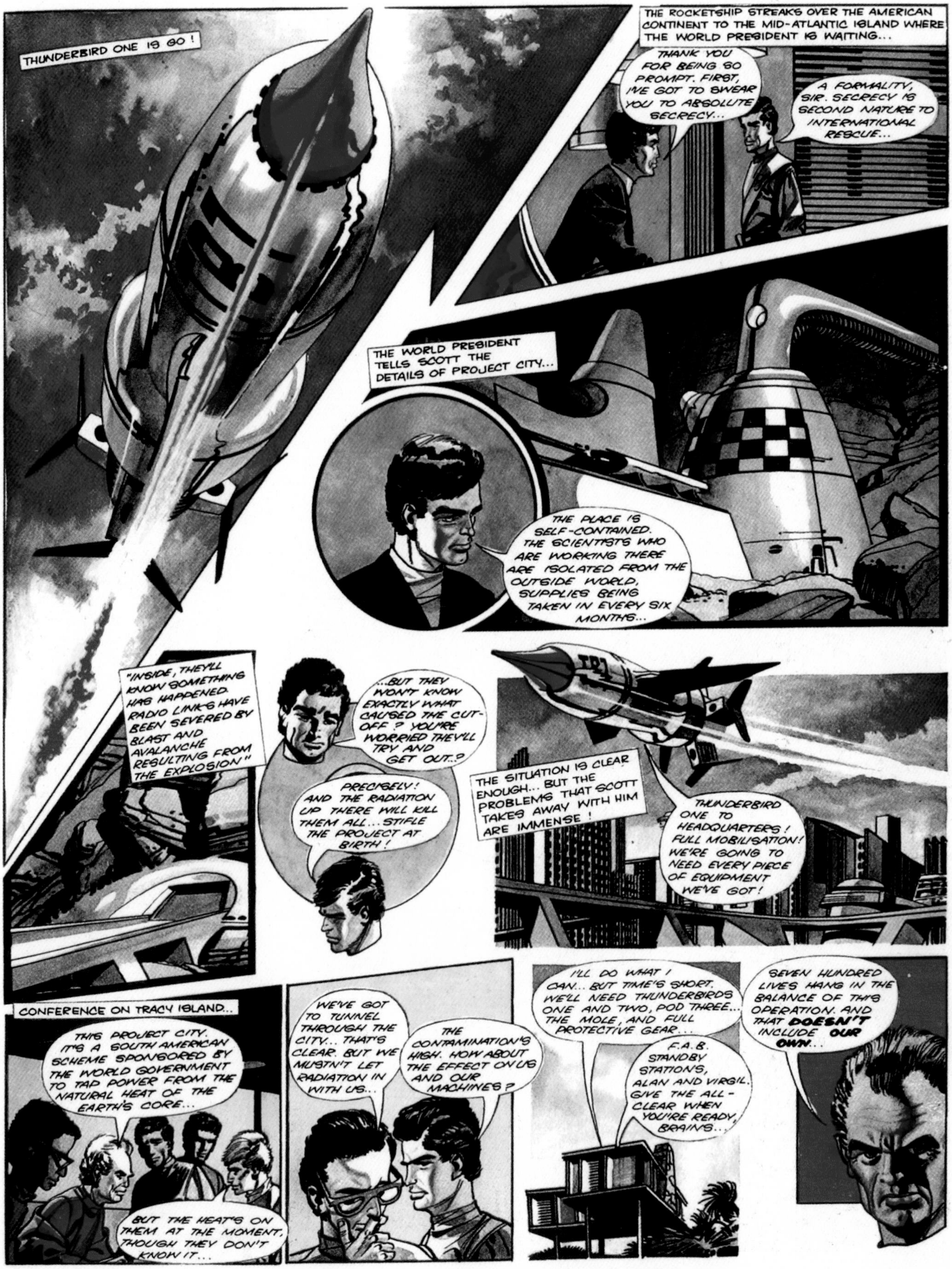
THUNDERBIRD ONE IS GO!
THE ROCKETSHIP STREAKS OVER THE AMERICAN CONTINENT TO THE MID-ATLANTIC ISLAND WHERE THE WORLD PRESIDENT IS WAITING...
THANK YOU FOR BEING SO PROMPT. FIRST, I'VE GOT TO SWEAR YOU TO ABSOLUTE SECRECY...
A FORMALITY, SIR. SECRECY IS SECOND NATURE TO INTERNATIONAL RESCUE...
THE WORLD PRESIDENT TELLS SCOTT THE DETAILS OF PROJECT CITY...
THE PLACE IS SELF-CONTAINED. THE SCIENTISTS WHO ARE WORKING THERE ARE ISOLATED FROM THE OUTSIDE WORLD, SUPPLIES BEING TAKEN IN EVERY SIX MONTHS...
"INSIDE, THEY'LL KNOW SOMETHING HAS HAPPENED. RADIO LINKS HAVE BEEN SEVERED BY BLAST AND AVALANCHE RESULTING FROM THE EXPLOSION"
...BUT THEY WON'T KNOW EXACTLY WHAT CAUSED THE CUT-OFF? YOU'RE WORRIED THEY'LL TRY AND GET OUT..?
PRECISELY! AND THE RADIATION UP THERE WILL KILL THEM ALL... STIFLE THE PROJECT AT BIRTH!
THE SITUATION IS CLEAR ENOUGH... BUT THE PROBLEMS THAT SCOTT TAKES AWAY WITH HIM ARE IMMENSE!
THUNDERBIRD ONE TO HEADQUARTERS! FULL MOBILISATION! WE'RE GOING TO NEED EVERY PIECE OF EQUIPMENT WE'VE GOT!
CONFERENCE ON TRACY ISLAND...
THIS PROJECT CITY. IT'S A SOUTH AMERICAN SCHEME SPONSORED BY THE WORLD GOVERNMENT TO TAP POWER FROM THE NATURAL HEAT OF THE EARTH'S CORE...
BUT THE HEAT'S ON THEM AT THE MOMENT, THOUGH THEY DON'T KNOW IT...
WE'VE GOT TO TUNNEL THROUGH THE CITY... THAT'S CLEAR. BUT WE MUSTN'T LET RADIATION IN WITH US...
THE CONTAMINATION'S HIGH. HOW ABOUT THE EFFECT ON US AND OUR MACHINES?
I'LL DO WHAT I CAN... BUT TIME'S SHORT. WE'LL NEED THUNDERBIRDS ONE AND TWO, POD THREE... THE MOLE, AND FULL PROTECTIVE GEAR...
F.A.B. STANDBY STATIONS, ALAN AND VIRGIL. GIVE THE ALL-CLEAR WHEN YOU'RE READY, BRAINS...
SEVEN HUNDRED LIVES HANG IN THE BALANCE OF THIS OPERATION. AND THAT DOESN'T INCLUDE OUR OWN...

THUNDERBIRDS

Part 3 - dateline 05 April 2069

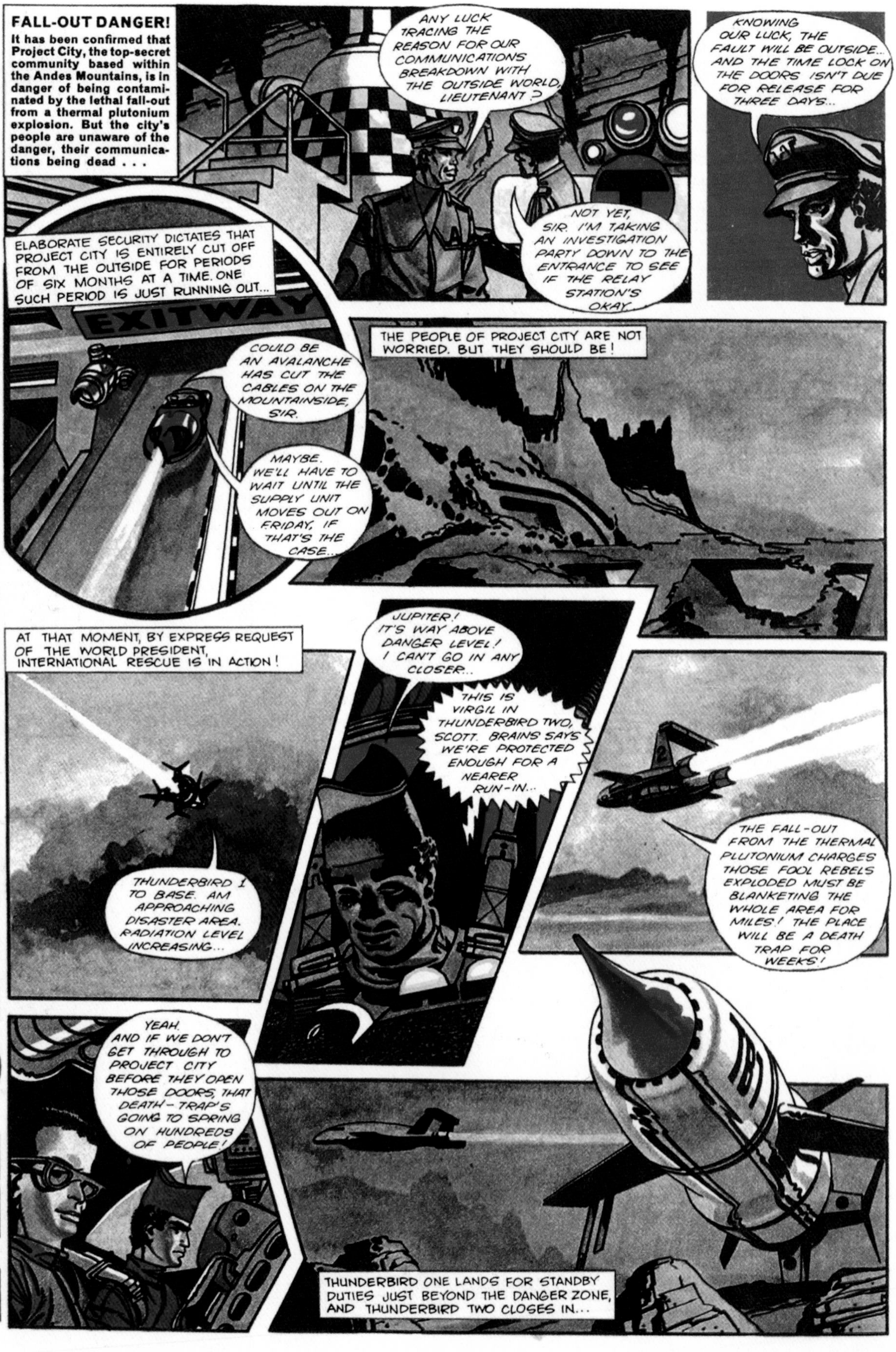
FALL-OUT DANGER!
It has been confirmed that Project City, the top-secret community based within the Andes Mountains, is in danger of being contaminated by the lethal fall-out from a thermal plutonium explosion. But the city's people are unaware of the danger, their communications being dead . . .
ANY LUCK TRACING THE REASON FOR OUR COMMUNICATIONS BREAKDOWN WITH THE OUTSIDE WORLD, LIEUTENANT?
NOT YET, SIR. I'M TAKING AN INVESTIGATION PARTY DOWN TO THE ENTRANCE TO SEE IF THE RELAY STATION'S OKAY.
KNOWING OUR LUCK, THE FAULT WILL BE OUTSIDE... AND THE TIME LOCK ON THE DOORS ISN'T DUE FOR RELEASE FOR THREE DAYS...
ELABORATE SECURITY DICTATES THAT PROJECT CITY IS ENTIRELY CUT OFF FROM THE OUTSIDE FOR PERIODS OF SIX MONTHS AT A TIME. ONE SUCH PERIOD IS JUST RUNNING OUT...
EXITWAY
COULD BE AN AVALANCHE HAS CUT THE CABLES ON THE MOUNTAINSIDE, SIR.
MAYBE. WE'LL HAVE TO WAIT UNTIL THE SUPPLY UNIT MOVES OUT ON FRIDAY, IF THAT'S THE CASE...
THE PEOPLE OF PROJECT CITY ARE NOT WORRIED. BUT THEY SHOULD BE!
AT THAT MOMENT, BY EXPRESS REQUEST OF THE WORLD PRESIDENT, INTERNATIONAL RESCUE IS IN ACTION!
THUNDERBIRD 1 TO BASE. AM APPROACHING DISASTER AREA. RADIATION LEVEL INCREASING...
JUPITER! IT'S WAY ABOVE DANGER LEVEL! I CAN'T GO IN ANY CLOSER...
THIS IS VIRGIL IN THUNDERBIRD TWO, SCOTT. BRAINS SAYS WE'RE PROTECTED ENOUGH FOR A NEARER RUN-IN...
THE FALL-OUT FROM THE THERMAL PLUTONIUM CHARGES THOSE FOOL REBELS EXPLODED MUST BE BLANKETING THE WHOLE AREA FOR MILES! THE PLACE WILL BE A DEATH TRAP FOR WEEKS!
YEAH. AND IF WE DON'T GET THROUGH TO PROJECT CITY BEFORE THEY OPEN THOSE DOORS, THAT DEATH-TRAP'S GOING TO SPRING ON HUNDREDS OF PEOPLE!
THUNDERBIRD ONE LANDS FOR STANDBY DUTIES JUST BEYOND THE DANGER ZONE, AND THUNDERBIRD TWO CLOSES IN...

Artist: Frank Bellamy

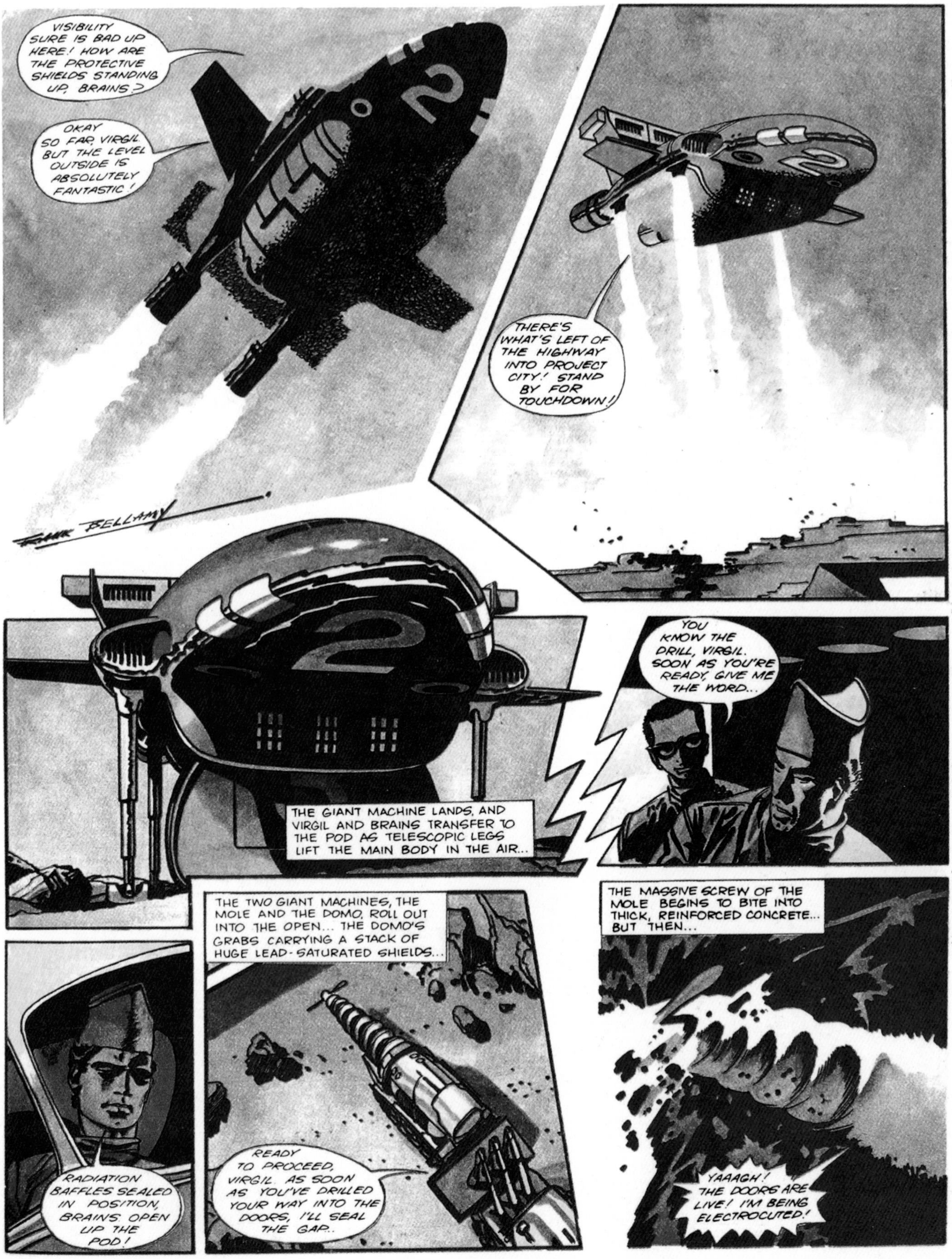
VISIBILITY SURE IS BAD UP HERE! HOW ARE THE PROTECTIVE SHIELDS STANDING UP, BRAINS?
OKAY SO FAR, VIRGIL. BUT THE LEVEL OUTSIDE IS ABSOLUTELY FANTASTIC!
THERE'S WHAT'S LEFT OF THE HIGHWAY INTO PROJECT CITY! STAND BY FOR TOUCHDOWN!
THE GIANT MACHINE LANDS, AND VIRGIL AND BRAINS TRANSFER TO THE POD AS TELESCOPIC LEGS LIFT THE MAIN BODY IN THE AIR...
YOU KNOW THE DRILL, VIRGIL. SOON AS YOU'RE READY, GIVE ME THE WORD...
RADIATION BAFFLES SEALED IN POSITION, BRAINS. OPEN UP THE POD!
THE TWO GIANT MACHINES, THE MOLE AND THE DOMO, ROLL OUT INTO THE OPEN... THE DOMO'S GRABS CARRYING A STACK OF HUGE LEAD-SATURATED SHIELDS...
READY TO PROCEED, VIRGIL. AS SOON AS YOU'VE DRILLED YOUR WAY INTO THE DOORS, I'LL SEAL THE GAP...
THE MASSIVE SCREW OF THE MOLE BEGINS TO BITE INTO THICK, REINFORCED CONCRETE... BUT THEN...
YAAAGH! THE DOORS ARE LIVE! I'M BEING ELECTROCUTED!

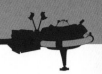

Part 4 - dateline 12 April 2069

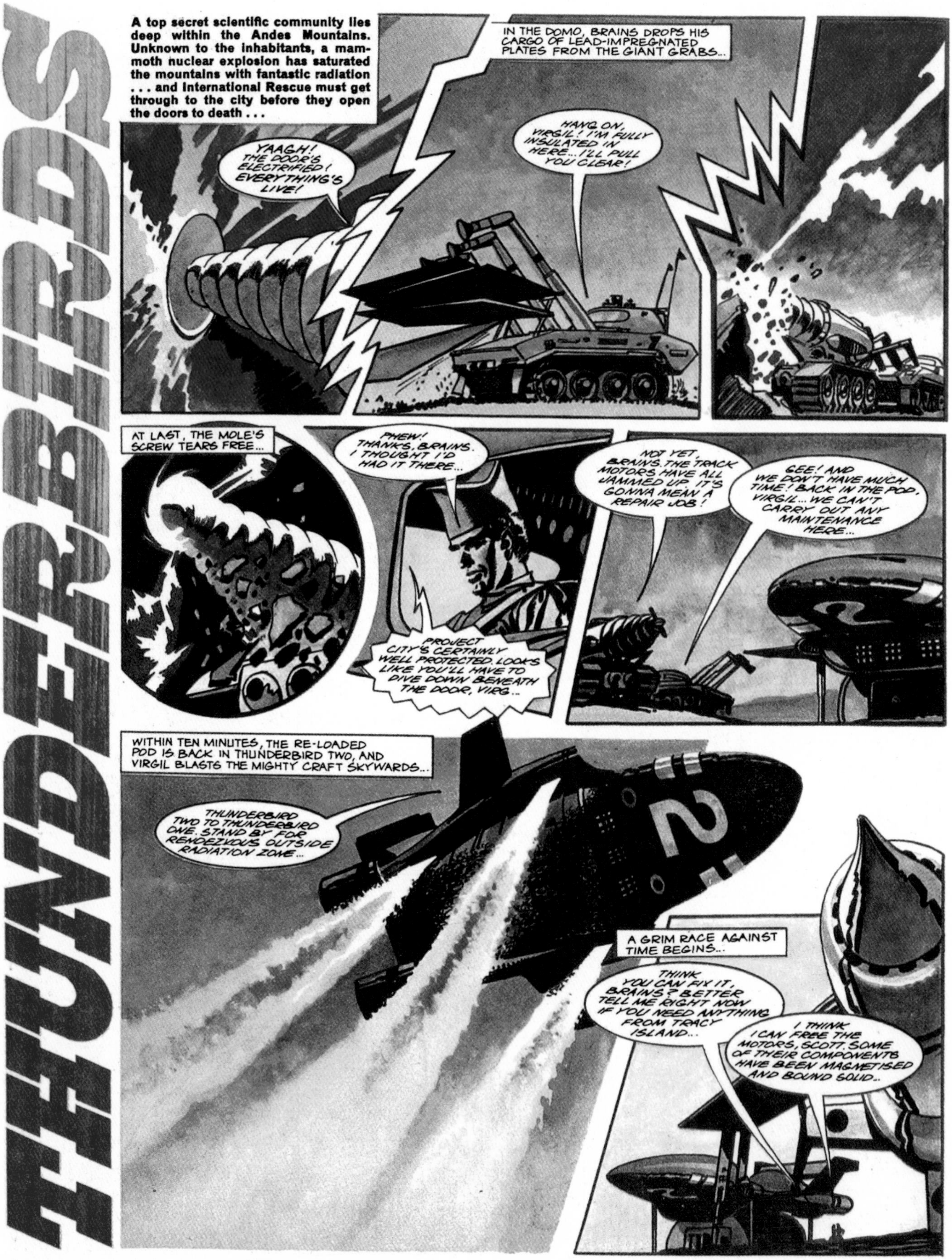
THUNDERBIRDS
A top secret scientific community lies deep within the Andes Mountains. Unknown to the inhabitants, a mammoth nuclear explosion has saturated the mountains with fantastic radiation . . . and International Rescue must get through to the city before they open the doors to death . . .
IN THE DOMO, BRAINS DROPS HIS CARGO OF LEAD-IMPREGNATED PLATES FROM THE GIANT GRABS...
YAAGH! THE DOOR'S ELECTRIFIED! EVERYTHING'S LIVE!
HANG ON, VIRGIL! I'M FULLY INSULATED IN HERE... I'LL PULL YOU CLEAR!
AT LAST, THE MOLE'S SCREW TEARS FREE...
PHEW! THANKS, BRAINS. I THOUGHT I'D HAD IT THERE...
PROJECT CITY'S CERTAINLY WELL PROTECTED. LOOKS LIKE YOU'LL HAVE TO DIVE DOWN BENEATH THE DOOR, VIRG...
NOT YET, BRAINS. THE TRACK MOTORS HAVE ALL JAMMED UP. IT'S GONNA MEAN A REPAIR JOB!
GEE! AND WE DON'T HAVE MUCH TIME! BACK IN THE POD, VIRGIL... WE CAN'T CARRY OUT ANY MAINTENANCE HERE...
WITHIN TEN MINUTES, THE RE-LOADED POD IS BACK IN THUNDERBIRD TWO, AND VIRGIL BLASTS THE MIGHTY CRAFT SKYWARDS...
THUNDERBIRD TWO TO THUNDERBIRD ONE. STAND BY FOR RENDEZVOUS OUTSIDE RADIATION ZONE...
A GRIM RACE AGAINST TIME BEGINS...
THINK YOU CAN FIX IT, BRAINS? BETTER TELL ME RIGHT NOW IF YOU NEED ANYTHING FROM TRACY ISLAND...
I THINK I CAN FREE THE MOTORS, SCOTT. SOME OF THEIR COMPONENTS HAVE BEEN MAGNETISED AND BOUND SOLID...

Artist: Frank Bellamy

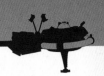

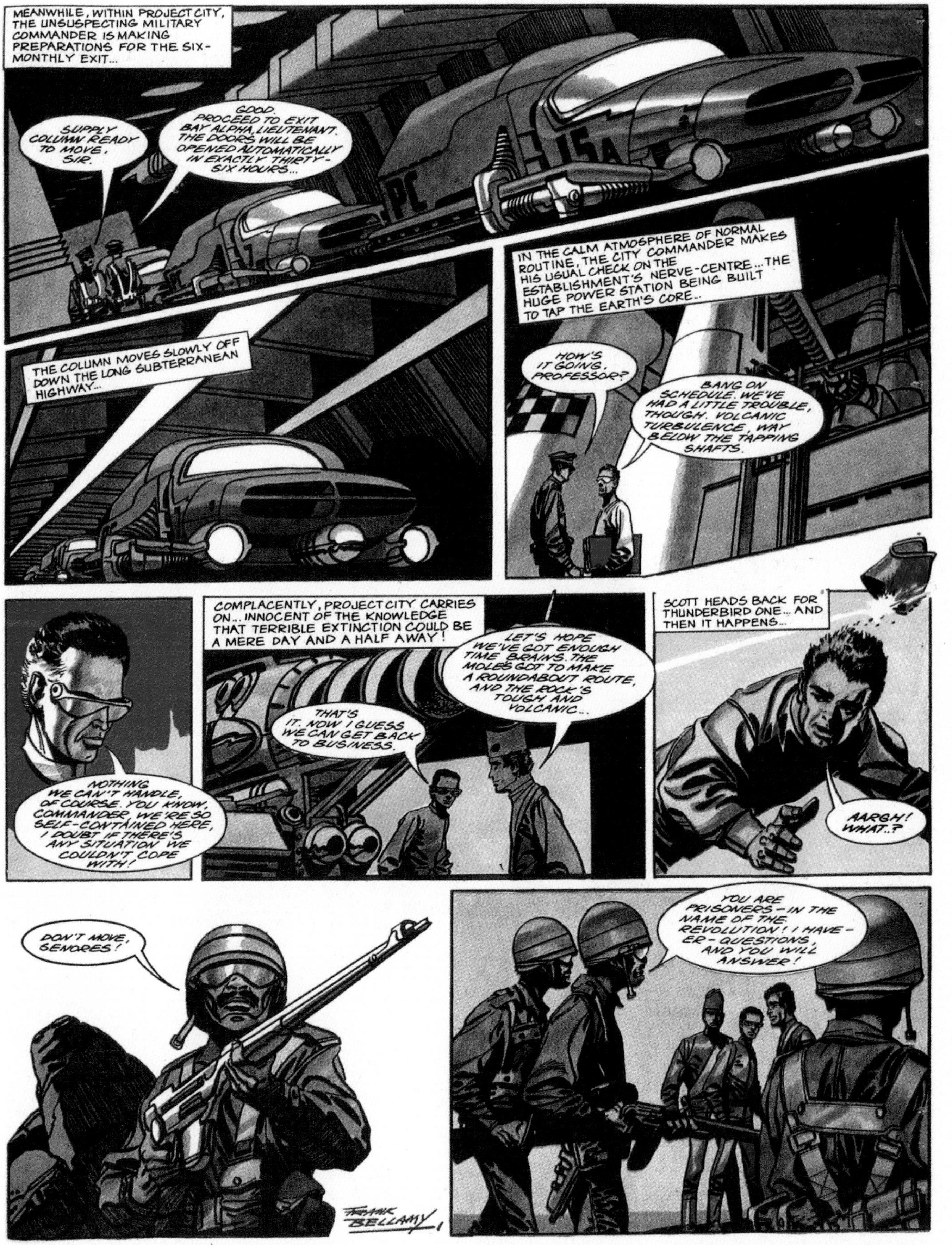
MEANWHILE, WITHIN PROJECT CITY, THE UNSUSPECTING MILITARY COMMANDER IS MAKING PREPARATIONS FOR THE SIX-MONTHLY EXIT...
SUPPLY COLUMN READY TO MOVE, SIR.
GOOD. PROCEED TO EXIT BAY ALPHA, LIEUTENANT. THE DOORS WILL BE OPENED AUTOMATICALLY IN EXACTLY THIRTY-SIX HOURS...
15A
PC
THE COLUMN MOVES SLOWLY OFF DOWN THE LONG SUBTERRANEAN HIGHWAY...
IN THE CALM ATMOSPHERE OF NORMAL ROUTINE, THE CITY COMMANDER MAKES HIS USUAL CHECK ON THE ESTABLISHMENT'S NERVE-CENTRE... THE HUGE POWER STATION BEING BUILT TO TAP THE EARTH'S CORE...
HOW'S IT GOING, PROFESSOR?
BANG ON SCHEDULE. WE'VE HAD A LITTLE TROUBLE, THOUGH. VOLCANIC TURBULENCE, WAY BELOW THE TAPPING SHAFTS.
NOTHING WE CAN'T HANDLE, OF COURSE. YOU KNOW, COMMANDER, WE'RE SO SELF-CONTAINED HERE, I DOUBT IF THERE'S ANY SITUATION WE COULDN'T COPE WITH!
COMPLACENTLY, PROJECT CITY CARRIES ON... INNOCENT OF THE KNOWLEDGE THAT TERRIBLE EXTINCTION COULD BE A MERE DAY AND A HALF AWAY!
LET'S HOPE WE'VE GOT ENOUGH TIME BRAINS. THE MOLE'S GOT TO MAKE A ROUNDABOUT ROUTE, AND THE ROCK'S TOUGH AND VOLCANIC...
THAT'S IT. NOW I GUESS WE CAN GET BACK TO BUSINESS.
SCOTT HEADS BACK FOR THUNDERBIRD ONE... AND THEN IT HAPPENS...
AARGH! WHAT..?
DON'T MOVE, SENORES!
YOU ARE PRISONERS — IN THE NAME OF THE REVOLUTION! I HAVE — ER — QUESTIONS, AND YOU WILL ANSWER!
FRANK BELLAMY

Part 5 - dateline 19 April 2069

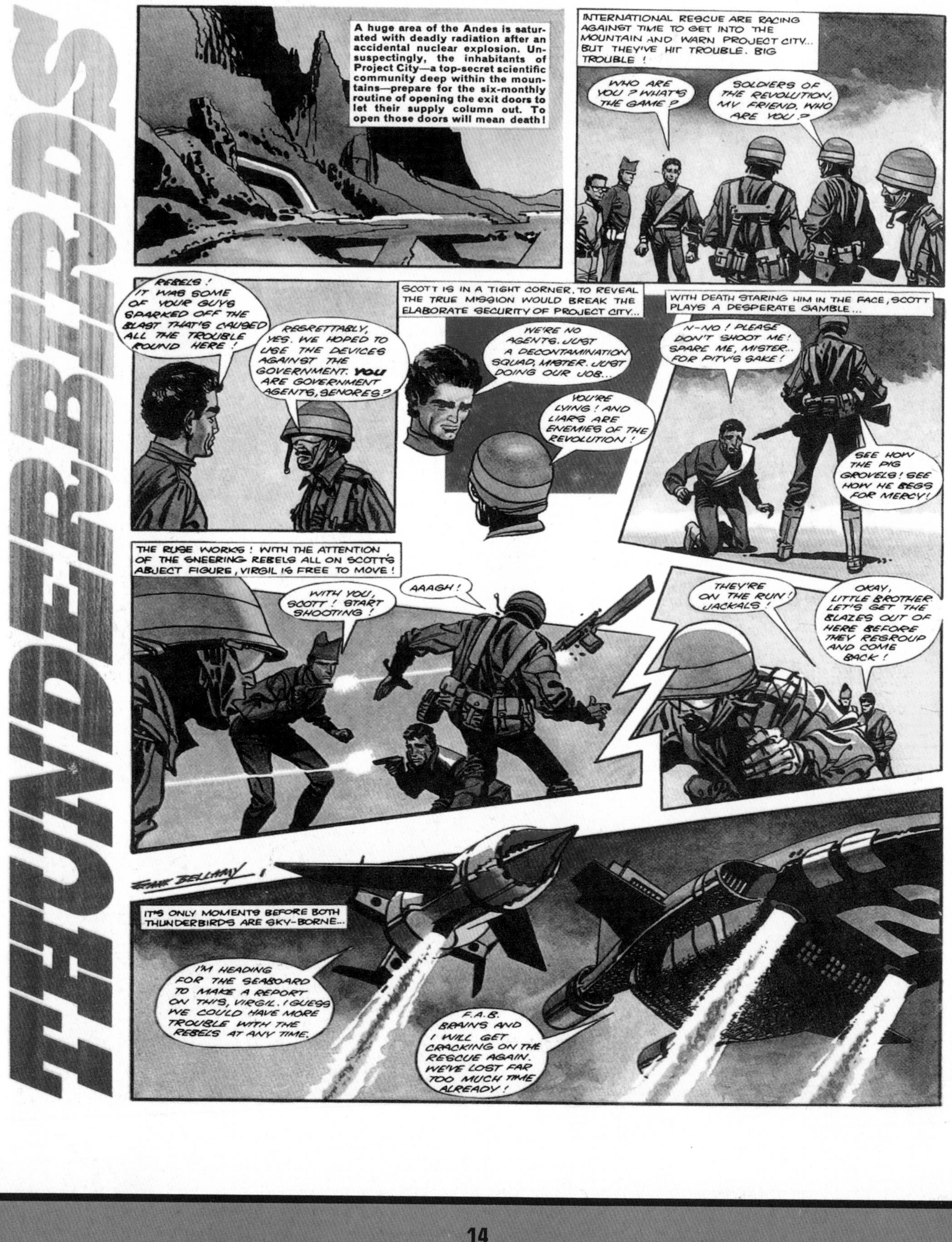
THUNDERBIRDS
A huge area of the Andes is saturated with deadly radiation after an accidental nuclear explosion. Unsuspectingly, the inhabitants of Project City—a top-secret scientific community deep within the mountains—prepare for the six-monthly routine of opening the exit doors to let their supply column out. To open those doors will mean death!
INTERNATIONAL RESCUE ARE RACING AGAINST TIME TO GET INTO THE MOUNTAIN AND WARN PROJECT CITY... BUT THEY'VE HIT TROUBLE. BIG TROUBLE!
WHO ARE YOU? WHAT'S THE GAME?
SOLDIERS OF THE REVOLUTION, MY FRIEND. WHO ARE YOU?
REBELS! IT WAS SOME OF YOUR GUYS SPARKED OFF THE BLAST THAT'S CAUSED ALL THE TROUBLE ROUND HERE!
REGRETTABLY, YES. WE HOPED TO USE THE DEVICES AGAINST THE GOVERNMENT. YOU ARE GOVERNMENT AGENTS, SENORES?
SCOTT IS IN A TIGHT CORNER. TO REVEAL THE TRUE MISSION WOULD BREAK THE ELABORATE SECURITY OF PROJECT CITY...
WE'RE NO AGENTS. JUST A DECONTAMINATION SQUAD, MISTER. JUST DOING OUR JOB...
YOU'RE LYING! AND LIARS ARE ENEMIES OF THE REVOLUTION!
WITH DEATH STARING HIM IN THE FACE, SCOTT PLAYS A DESPERATE GAMBLE...
N-NO! PLEASE DON'T SHOOT ME! SPARE ME, MISTER... FOR PITY'S SAKE!
SEE HOW THE PIG GROVELS! SEE HOW HE BEGS FOR MERCY!
THE RUSE WORKS! WITH THE ATTENTION OF THE SNEERING REBELS ALL ON SCOTT'S ABJECT FIGURE, VIRGIL IS FREE TO MOVE!
WITH YOU, SCOTT! START SHOOTING!
AAAGH!
THEY'RE ON THE RUN! JACKALS!
OKAY, LITTLE BROTHER. LET'S GET THE BLAZES OUT OF HERE BEFORE THEY REGROUP AND COME BACK!
FRANK BELLAMY
IT'S ONLY MOMENTS BEFORE BOTH THUNDERBIRDS ARE SKY-BORNE...
I'M HEADING FOR THE SEABOARD TO MAKE A REPORT ON THIS, VIRGIL. I GUESS WE COULD HAVE MORE TROUBLE WITH THE REBELS AT ANY TIME.
F.A.B. BRAINS AND I WILL GET CRACKING ON THE RESCUE AGAIN. WE'VE LOST FAR TOO MUCH TIME ALREADY!

Artist: Frank Bellamy

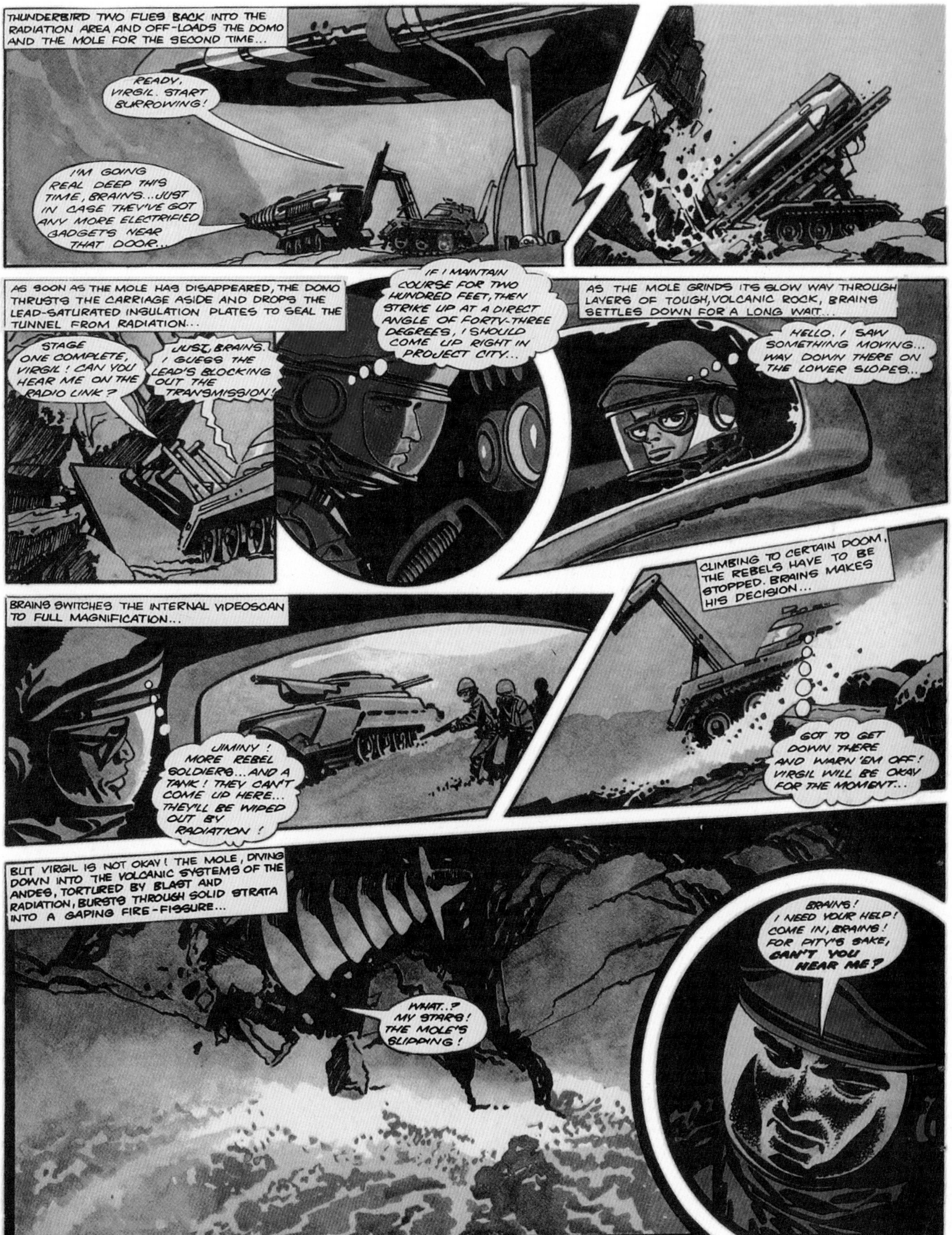
THUNDERBIRD TWO FLIES BACK INTO THE RADIATION AREA AND OFF-LOADS THE DOMO AND THE MOLE FOR THE SECOND TIME...
READY, VIRGIL. START BURROWING!
I'M GOING REAL DEEP THIS TIME, BRAINS... JUST IN CASE THEY'VE GOT ANY MORE ELECTRIFIED GADGETS NEAR THAT DOOR...
AS SOON AS THE MOLE HAS DISAPPEARED, THE DOMO THRUSTS THE CARRIAGE ASIDE AND DROPS THE LEAD-SATURATED INSULATION PLATES TO SEAL THE TUNNEL FROM RADIATION...
STAGE ONE COMPLETE, VIRGIL! CAN YOU HEAR ME ON THE RADIO LINK?
JUST, BRAINS. I GUESS THE LEAD'S BLOCKING OUT THE TRANSMISSION!
IF I MAINTAIN COURSE FOR TWO HUNDRED FEET, THEN STRIKE UP AT A DIRECT ANGLE OF FORTY-THREE DEGREES, I SHOULD COME UP RIGHT IN PROJECT CITY...
AS THE MOLE GRINDS ITS SLOW WAY THROUGH LAYERS OF TOUGH, VOLCANIC ROCK, BRAINS SETTLES DOWN FOR A LONG WAIT...
HELLO. I SAW SOMETHING MOVING... WAY DOWN THERE ON THE LOWER SLOPES...
BRAINS SWITCHES THE INTERNAL VIDEOSCAN TO FULL MAGNIFICATION...
JIMINY! MORE REBEL SOLDIERS... AND A TANK! THEY CAN'T COME UP HERE... THEY'LL BE WIPED OUT BY RADIATION!
CLIMBING TO CERTAIN DOOM, THE REBELS HAVE TO BE STOPPED. BRAINS MAKES HIS DECISION...
GOT TO GET DOWN THERE AND WARN 'EM OFF! VIRGIL WILL BE OKAY FOR THE MOMENT...
BUT VIRGIL IS NOT OKAY! THE MOLE, DIVING DOWN INTO THE VOLCANIC SYSTEMS OF THE ANDES, TORTURED BY BLAST AND RADIATION, BURSTS THROUGH SOLID STRATA INTO A GAPING FIRE-FISSURE...
WHAT..? MY STARS! THE MOLE'S SLIPPING!
BRAINS! I NEED YOUR HELP! COME IN, BRAINS! FOR PITY'S SAKE, CAN'T YOU HEAR ME?

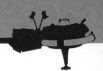

Part 6 - dateline 26 April 2069

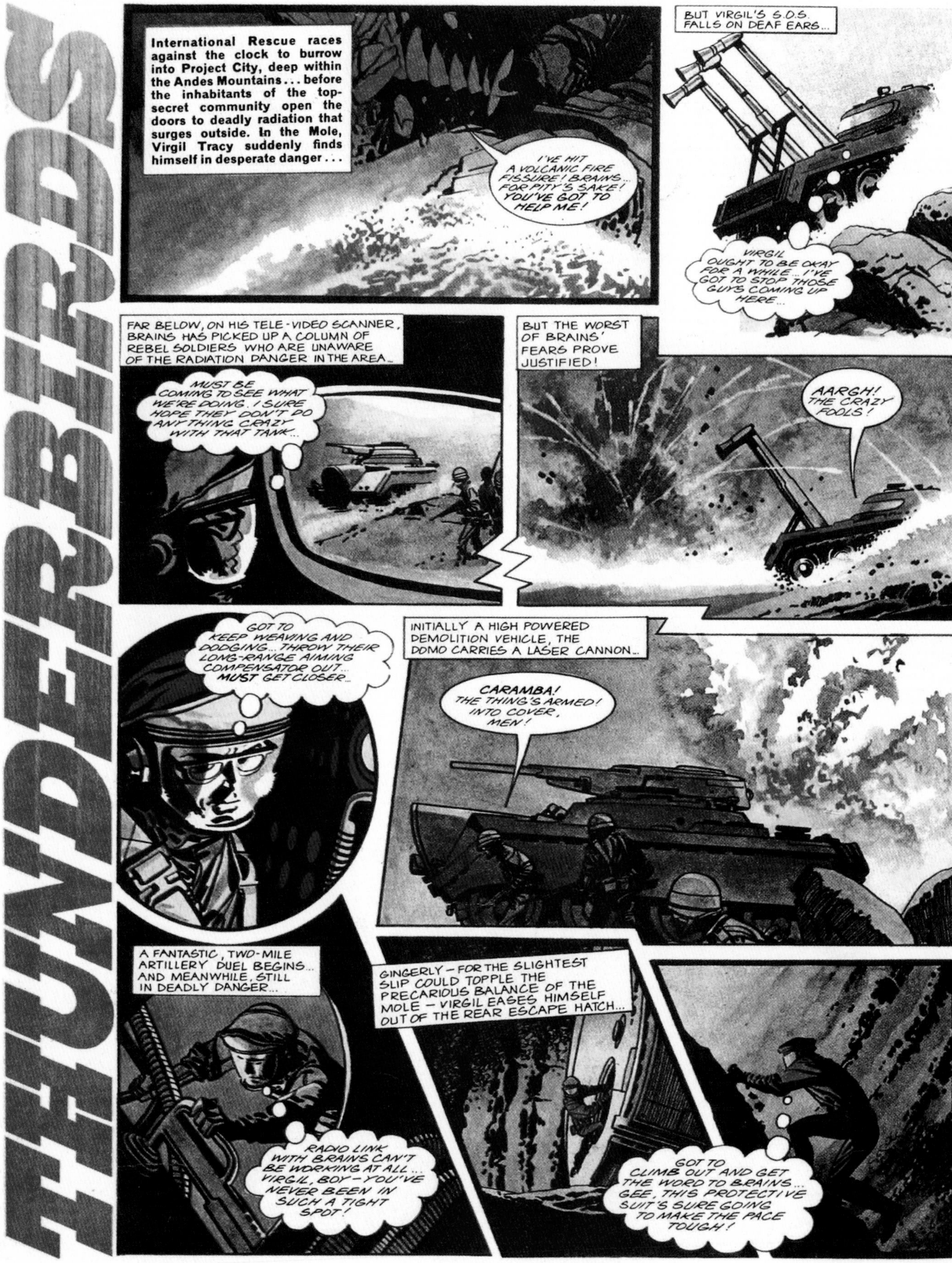
THUNDERBIRDS
International Rescue races against the clock to burrow into Project City, deep within the Andes Mountains . . . before the inhabitants of the top-secret community open the doors to deadly radiation that surges outside. In the Mole, Virgil Tracy suddenly finds himself in desperate danger . . .
I'VE HIT A VOLCANIC FIRE FISSURE! BRAINS... FOR PITY'S SAKE! YOU'VE GOT TO HELP ME!
BUT VIRGIL'S S.O.S. FALLS ON DEAF EARS...
VIRGIL OUGHT TO BE OKAY FOR A WHILE... I'VE GOT TO STOP THOSE GUYS COMING UP HERE...
FAR BELOW, ON HIS TELE-VIDEO SCANNER, BRAINS HAS PICKED UP A COLUMN OF REBEL SOLDIERS WHO ARE UNAWARE OF THE RADIATION DANGER IN THE AREA...
MUST BE COMING TO SEE WHAT WE'RE DOING. I SURE HOPE THEY DON'T DO ANYTHING CRAZY WITH THAT TANK...
BUT THE WORST OF BRAINS' FEARS PROVE JUSTIFIED!
AARGH! THE CRAZY FOOLS!
GOT TO KEEP WEAVING AND DODGING... THROW THEIR LONG-RANGE AIMING COMPENSATOR OUT... MUST GET CLOSER...
INITIALLY A HIGH POWERED DEMOLITION VEHICLE, THE DOMO CARRIES A LASER CANNON...
CARAMBA! THE THING'S ARMED! INTO COVER, MEN!
A FANTASTIC, TWO-MILE ARTILLERY DUEL BEGINS... AND MEANWHILE, STILL IN DEADLY DANGER...
RADIO LINK WITH BRAINS CAN'T BE WORKING AT ALL... VIRGIL, BOY - YOU'VE NEVER BEEN IN SUCH A TIGHT SPOT!
GINGERLY - FOR THE SLIGHTEST SLIP COULD TOPPLE THE PRECARIOUS BALANCE OF THE MOLE - VIRGIL EASES HIMSELF OUT OF THE REAR ESCAPE HATCH...
GOT TO CLIMB OUT AND GET THE WORD TO BRAINS... GEE, THIS PROTECTIVE SUIT'S SURE GOING TO MAKE THE PACE TOUGH!

Artist: Frank Bellamy

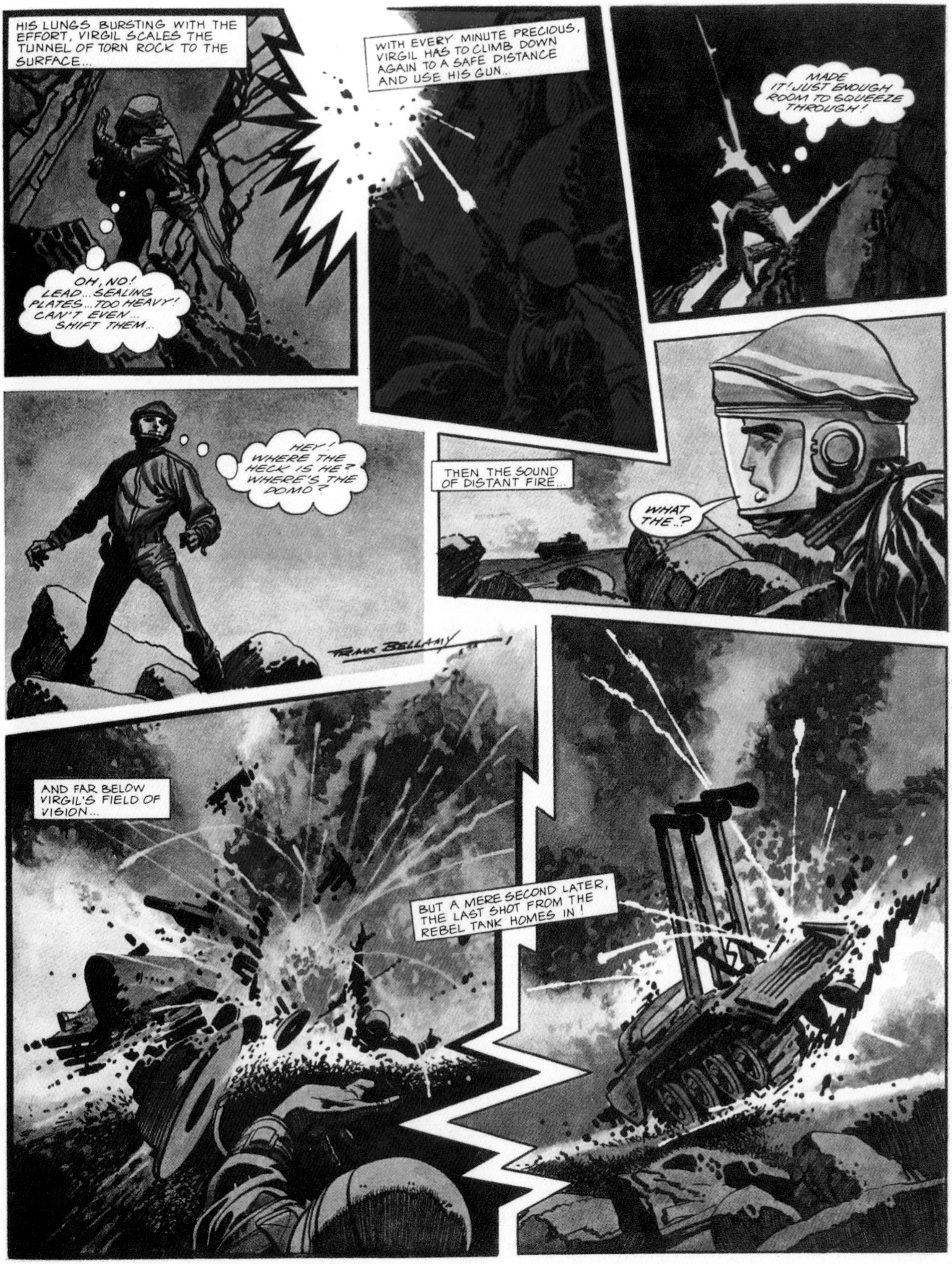
HIS LUNGS BURSTING WITH THE EFFORT, VIRGIL SCALES THE TUNNEL OF TORN ROCK TO THE SURFACE...
OH, NO! LEAD... SEALING PLATES... TOO HEAVY! CAN'T EVEN... SHIFT THEM...
WITH EVERY MINUTE PRECIOUS, VIRGIL HAS TO CLIMB DOWN AGAIN TO A SAFE DISTANCE AND USE HIS GUN...
MADE IT! JUST ENOUGH ROOM TO SQUEEZE THROUGH!
HEY! WHERE THE HECK IS HE? WHERE'S THE DOMO?
FRANK BELLAMY
THEN THE SOUND OF DISTANT FIRE...
WHAT THE..?
AND FAR BELOW VIRGIL'S FIELD OF VISION...
BUT A MERE SECOND LATER, THE LAST SHOT FROM THE REBEL TANK HOMES IN!

THUNDERBIRDS

Part 7 - dateline 03 May 2069

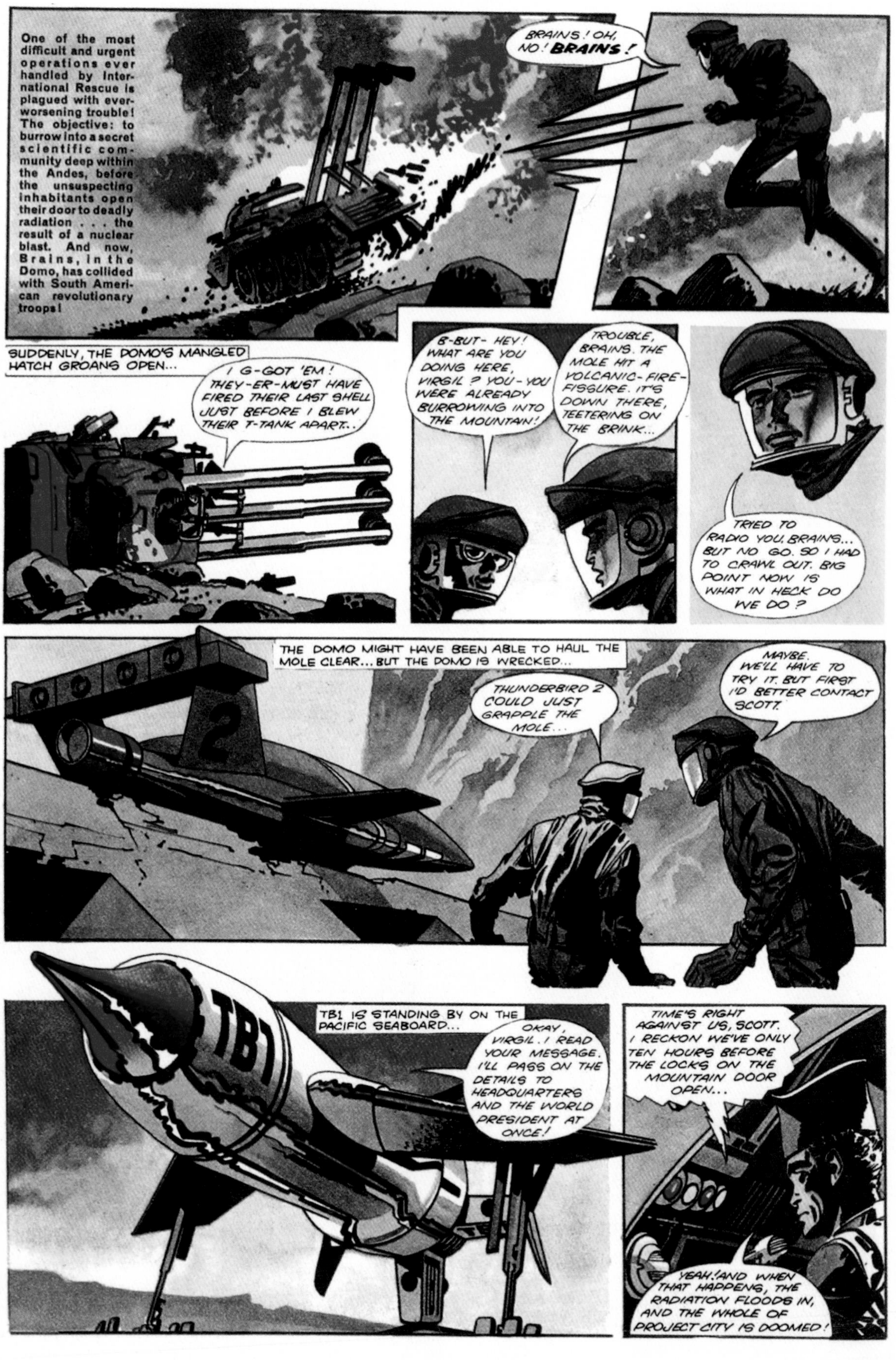
One of the most difficult and urgent operations ever handled by International Rescue is plagued with ever-worsening trouble! The objective: to burrow into a secret scientific community deep within the Andes, before the unsuspecting inhabitants open their door to deadly radiation . . . the result of a nuclear blast. And now, Brains, in the Domo, has collided with South American revolutionary troops!
BRAINS! OH, NO! BRAINS!
SUDDENLY, THE DOMO'S MANGLED HATCH GROANS OPEN...
I G-GOT 'EM! THEY-ER-MUST HAVE FIRED THEIR LAST SHELL JUST BEFORE I BLEW THEIR T-TANK APART..
B-BUT- HEY! WHAT ARE YOU DOING HERE, VIRGIL? YOU-YOU WERE ALREADY BURROWING INTO THE MOUNTAIN!
TROUBLE, BRAINS. THE MOLE HIT A VOLCANIC-FIRE-FISSURE. IT'S DOWN THERE, TEETERING ON THE BRINK...
TRIED TO RADIO YOU, BRAINS... BUT NO GO. SO I HAD TO CRAWL OUT. BIG POINT NOW IS WHAT IN HECK DO WE DO?
THE DOMO MIGHT HAVE BEEN ABLE TO HAUL THE MOLE CLEAR... BUT THE DOMO IS WRECKED...
THUNDERBIRD 2 COULD JUST GRAPPLE THE MOLE...
MAYBE. WE'LL HAVE TO TRY IT. BUT FIRST I'D BETTER CONTACT SCOTT.
TB1 IS STANDING BY ON THE PACIFIC SEABOARD...
OKAY, VIRGIL. I READ YOUR MESSAGE. I'LL PASS ON THE DETAILS TO HEADQUARTERS AND THE WORLD PRESIDENT AT ONCE!
TIME'S RIGHT AGAINST US, SCOTT. I RECKON WE'VE ONLY TEN HOURS BEFORE THE LOCKS ON THE MOUNTAIN DOOR OPEN...
YEAH! AND WHEN THAT HAPPENS, THE RADIATION FLOODS IN, AND THE WHOLE OF PROJECT CITY IS DOOMED!

Artist: Frank Bellamy

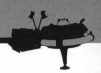

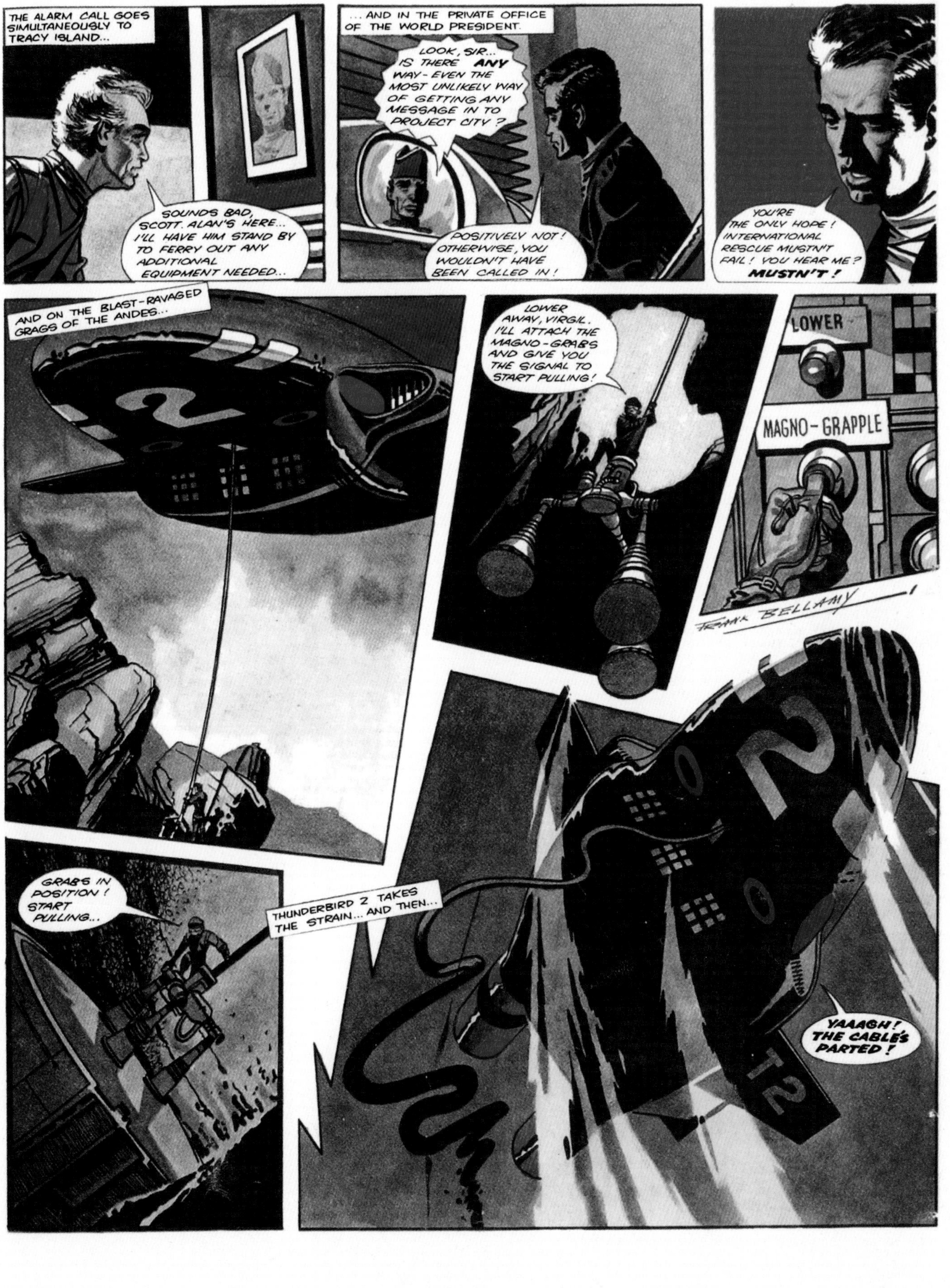
THE ALARM CALL GOES SIMULTANEOUSLY TO TRACY ISLAND...
SOUNDS BAD, SCOTT. ALAN'S HERE... I'LL HAVE HIM STAND BY TO FERRY OUT ANY ADDITIONAL EQUIPMENT NEEDED...
... AND IN THE PRIVATE OFFICE OF THE WORLD PRESIDENT.
LOOK, SIR... IS THERE ANY WAY - EVEN THE MOST UNLIKELY WAY OF GETTING ANY MESSAGE IN TO PROJECT CITY?
POSITIVELY NOT! OTHERWISE, YOU WOULDN'T HAVE BEEN CALLED IN!
YOU'RE THE ONLY HOPE! INTERNATIONAL RESCUE MUSTN'T FAIL! YOU HEAR ME? MUSTN'T!
AND ON THE BLAST-RAVAGED CRAGS OF THE ANDES...
LOWER AWAY, VIRGIL. I'LL ATTACH THE MAGNO-GRABS AND GIVE YOU THE SIGNAL TO START PULLING!
LOWER
MAGNO-GRAPPLE
FRANK BELLAMY
GRAB'S IN POSITION! START PULLING...
THUNDERBIRD 2 TAKES THE STRAIN... AND THEN...
YAAAGH! THE CABLE'S PARTED!
T2

Part 8 - dateline 10 May 2069

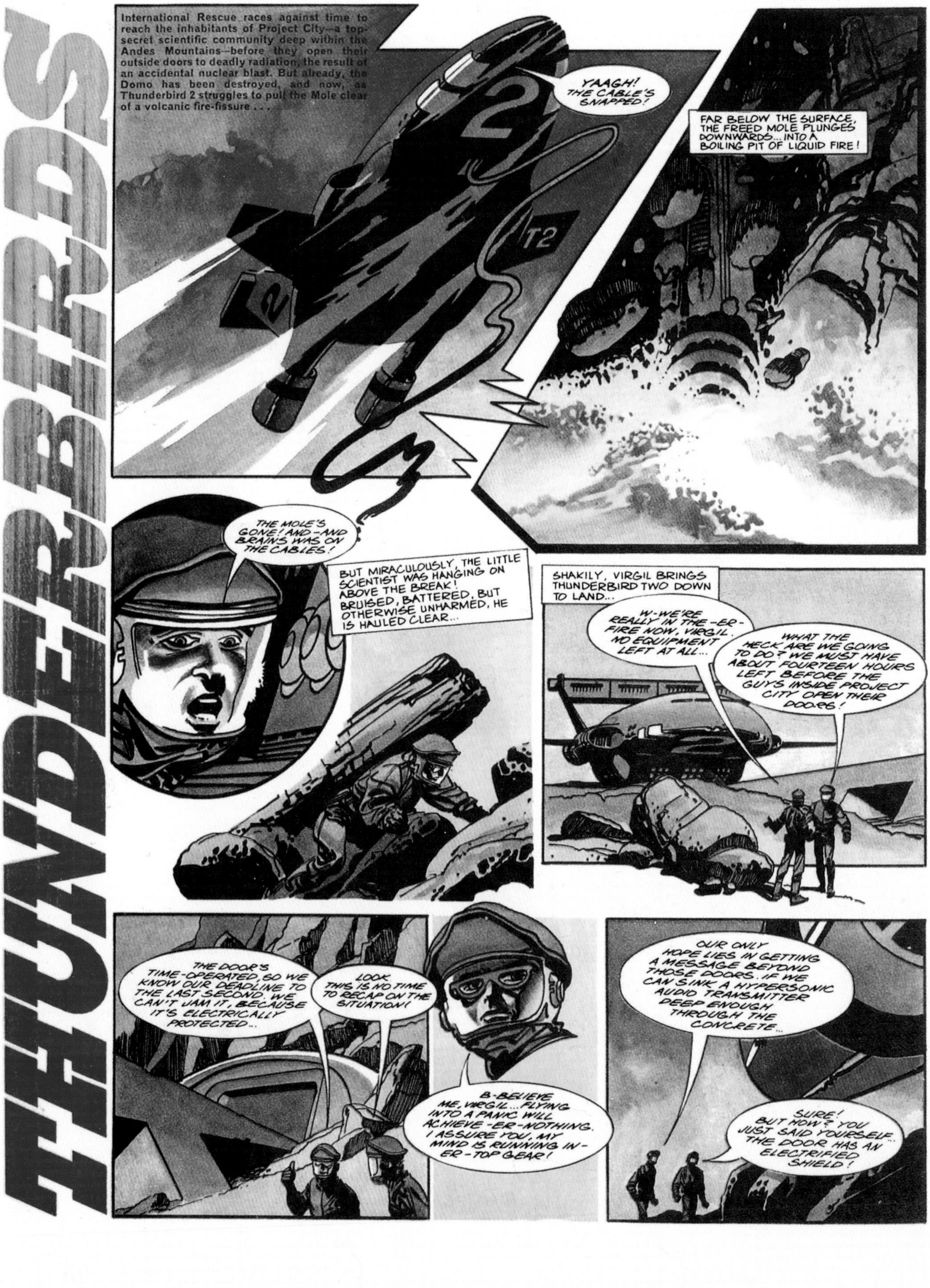
THUNDERBIRDS
International Rescue races against time to reach the inhabitants of Project City—a top-secret scientific community deep within the Andes Mountains—before they open their outside doors to deadly radiation, the result of an accidental nuclear blast. But already, the Domo has been destroyed, and now, as Thunderbird 2 struggles to pull the Mole clear of a volcanic fire-fissure . . .
YAAGH! THE CABLE'S SNAPPED!
FAR BELOW THE SURFACE, THE FREED MOLE PLUNGES DOWNWARDS... INTO A BOILING PIT OF LIQUID FIRE!
THE MOLE'S GONE! AND—AND BRAINS WAS ON THE CABLES!
BUT MIRACULOUSLY, THE LITTLE SCIENTIST WAS HANGING ON ABOVE THE BREAK! BRUISED, BATTERED, BUT OTHERWISE UNHARMED, HE IS HAULED CLEAR...
SHAKILY, VIRGIL BRINGS THUNDERBIRD TWO DOWN TO LAND...
W-WE'RE REALLY IN THE -ER FIRE NOW, VIRGIL. NO EQUIPMENT LEFT AT ALL...
WHAT THE HECK ARE WE GOING TO DO? WE MUST HAVE ABOUT FOURTEEN HOURS LEFT BEFORE THE GUYS INSIDE PROJECT CITY OPEN THEIR DOORS!
THE DOOR'S TIME-OPERATED, SO WE KNOW OUR DEADLINE TO THE LAST SECOND. WE CAN'T JAM IT, BECAUSE IT'S ELECTRICALLY PROTECTED...
LOOK, THIS IS NO TIME TO RECAP ON THE SITUATION!
B-BELIEVE ME, VIRGIL... FLYING INTO A PANIC WILL ACHIEVE -ER- NOTHING. I ASSURE YOU, MY MIND IS RUNNING IN- ER- TOP GEAR!
OUR ONLY HOPE LIES IN GETTING A MESSAGE BEYOND THOSE DOORS. IF WE CAN SINK A HYPERSONIC AUDIO TRANSMITTER DEEP ENOUGH THROUGH THE CONCRETE...
SURE! BUT HOW? YOU JUST SAID YOURSELF... THE DOOR HAS AN ELECTRIFIED SHIELD!

Artist: Frank Bellamy

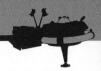

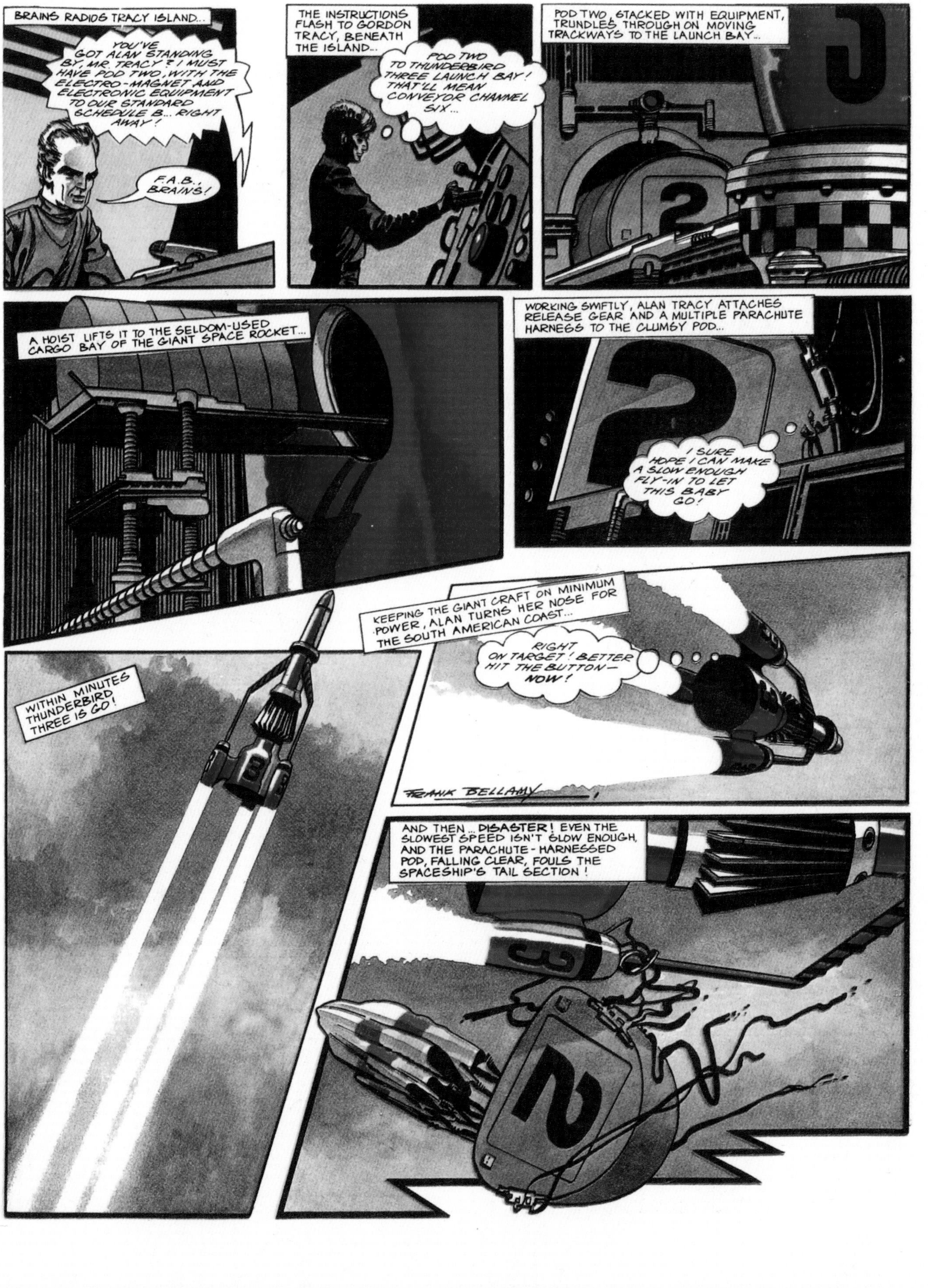
BRAINS RADIOS TRACY ISLAND...
YOU'VE GOT ALAN STANDING BY, MR. TRACY? I MUST HAVE POD TWO, WITH THE ELECTRO-MAGNET AND ELECTRONIC EQUIPMENT TO OUR STANDARD SCHEDULE B... RIGHT AWAY!
F.A.B., BRAINS!
THE INSTRUCTIONS FLASH TO GORDON TRACY, BENEATH THE ISLAND...
POD TWO TO THUNDERBIRD THREE LAUNCH BAY! THAT'LL MEAN CONVEYOR CHANNEL SIX...
POD TWO, STACKED WITH EQUIPMENT, TRUNDLES THROUGH ON MOVING TRACKWAYS TO THE LAUNCH BAY...
A HOIST LIFTS IT TO THE SELDOM-USED CARGO BAY OF THE GIANT SPACE ROCKET...
WORKING SWIFTLY, ALAN TRACY ATTACHES RELEASE GEAR AND A MULTIPLE PARACHUTE HARNESS TO THE CLUMSY POD...
I SURE HOPE I CAN MAKE A SLOW ENOUGH FLY-IN TO LET THIS BABY GO!
WITHIN MINUTES THUNDERBIRD THREE IS GO!
KEEPING THE GIANT CRAFT ON MINIMUM POWER, ALAN TURNS HER NOSE FOR THE SOUTH AMERICAN COAST...
RIGHT ON TARGET! BETTER HIT THE BUTTON— NOW!
FRANK BELLAMY
AND THEN... DISASTER! EVEN THE SLOWEST SPEED ISN'T SLOW ENOUGH, AND THE PARACHUTE-HARNESSED POD, FALLING CLEAR, FOULS THE SPACESHIP'S TAIL SECTION!

Part 9 - dateline 17 May 2069

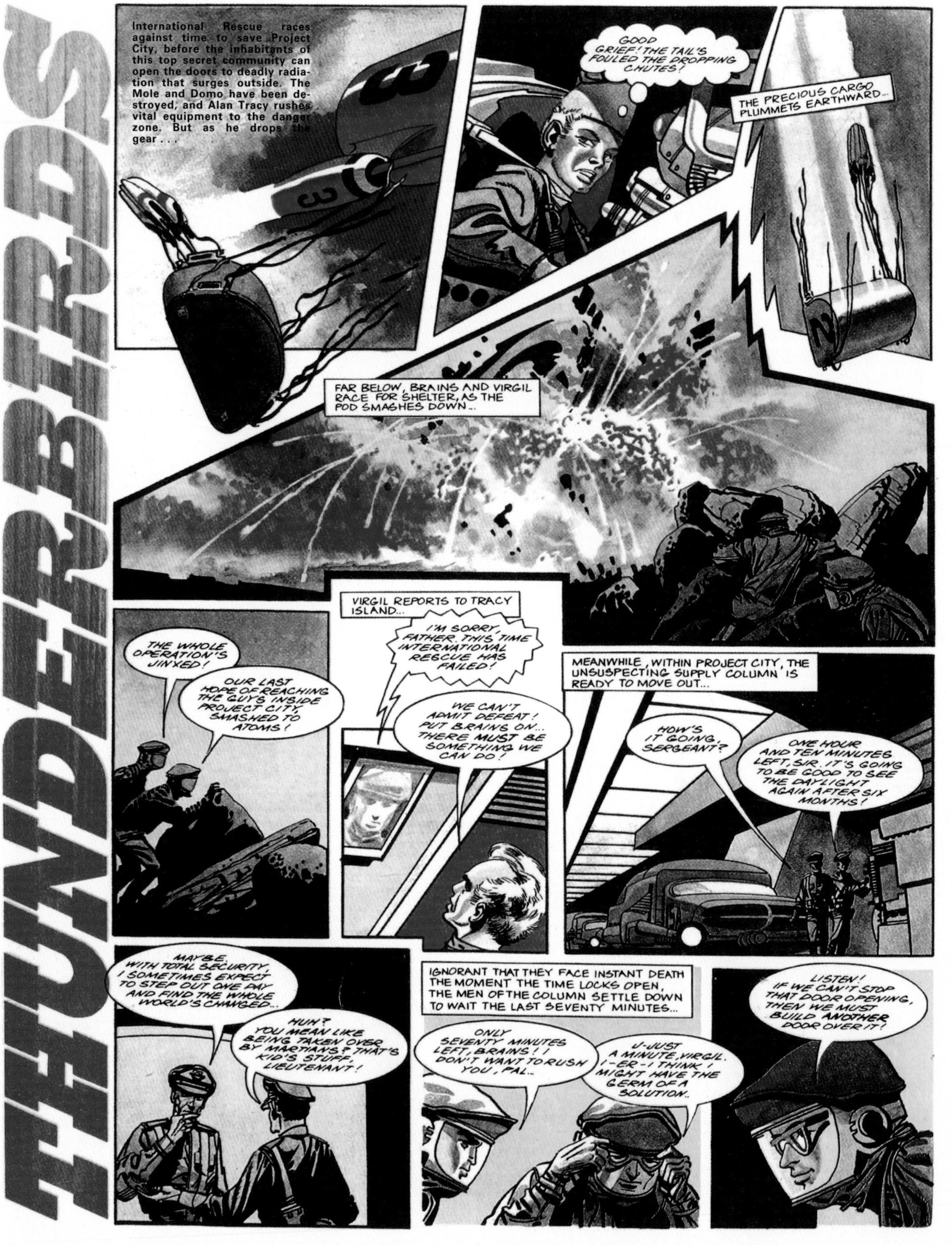
THUNDERBIRDS
International Rescue races against time to save Project City, before the inhabitants of this top secret community can open the doors to deadly radiation that surges outside. The Mole and Domo have been destroyed, and Alan Tracy rushes vital equipment to the danger zone. But as he drops the gear . . .
GOOD GRIEF! THE TAIL'S FOULED THE DROPPING CHUTES!
THE PRECIOUS CARGO PLUMMETS EARTHWARD...
FAR BELOW, BRAINS AND VIRGIL RACE FOR SHELTER, AS THE POD SMASHES DOWN...
THE WHOLE OPERATION'S JINXED!
OUR LAST HOPE OF REACHING THE GUYS INSIDE PROJECT CITY, SMASHED TO ATOMS!
VIRGIL REPORTS TO TRACY ISLAND...
I'M SORRY, FATHER. THIS TIME INTERNATIONAL RESCUE HAS FAILED!
WE CAN'T ADMIT DEFEAT! PUT BRAINS ON... THERE MUST BE SOMETHING WE CAN DO!
MEANWHILE, WITHIN PROJECT CITY, THE UNSUSPECTING SUPPLY COLUMN IS READY TO MOVE OUT...
HOW'S IT GOING, SERGEANT?
ONE HOUR AND TEN MINUTES LEFT, SIR. IT'S GOING TO BE GOOD TO SEE THE DAYLIGHT AGAIN AFTER SIX MONTHS!
MAYBE. WITH TOTAL SECURITY, I SOMETIMES EXPECT TO STEP OUT ONE DAY AND FIND THE WHOLE WORLD'S CHANGED...
HUH? YOU MEAN LIKE BEING TAKEN OVER BY MARTIANS? THAT'S KID'S STUFF, LIEUTENANT!
IGNORANT THAT THEY FACE INSTANT DEATH THE MOMENT THE TIME LOCKS OPEN, THE MEN OF THE COLUMN SETTLE DOWN TO WAIT THE LAST SEVENTY MINUTES...
ONLY SEVENTY MINUTES LEFT, BRAINS! I DON'T WANT TO RUSH YOU, PAL...
J-JUST A MINUTE, VIRGIL. I-ER-I THINK I MIGHT HAVE THE GERM OF A SOLUTION.
LISTEN! IF WE CAN'T STOP THAT DOOR OPENING, THEN WE MUST BUILD ANOTHER DOOR OVER IT!

Artist: Frank Bellamy

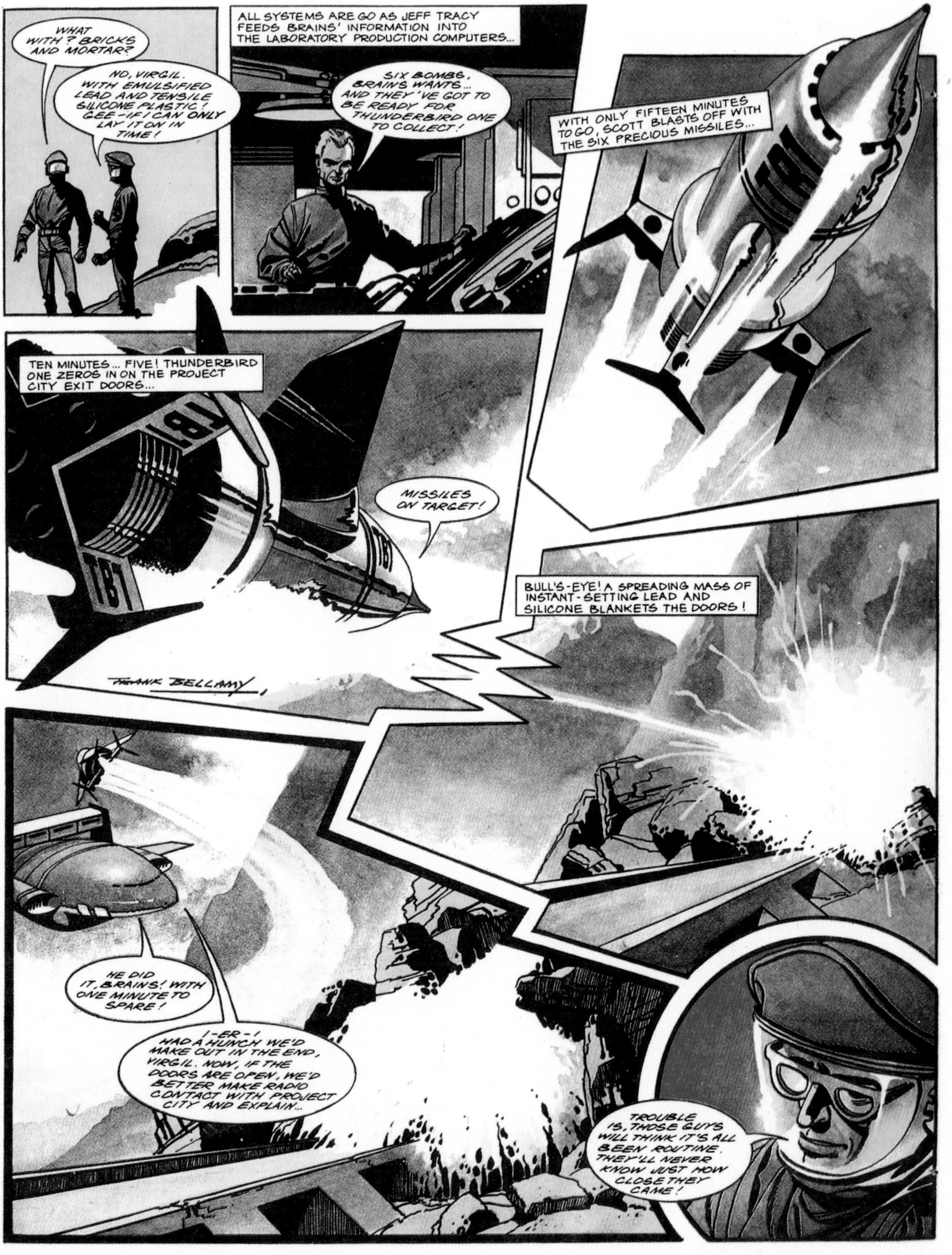
WHAT WITH? BRICKS AND MORTAR?
NO, VIRGIL. WITH EMULSIFIED LEAD AND TENSILE SILICONE PLASTIC! GEE-IF I CAN ONLY LAY IT ON IN TIME!
ALL SYSTEMS ARE GO AS JEFF TRACY FEEDS BRAINS' INFORMATION INTO THE LABORATORY PRODUCTION COMPUTERS...
SIX BOMBS, BRAINS WANTS... AND THEY'VE GOT TO BE READY FOR THUNDERBIRD ONE TO COLLECT!
WITH ONLY FIFTEEN MINUTES TO GO, SCOTT BLASTS OFF WITH THE SIX PRECIOUS MISSILES...
TB1
TEN MINUTES... FIVE! THUNDERBIRD ONE ZEROS IN ON THE PROJECT CITY EXIT DOORS...
TB1
MISSILES ON TARGET!
FRANK BELLAMY
BULL'S-EYE! A SPREADING MASS OF INSTANT-SETTING LEAD AND SILICONE BLANKETS THE DOORS!
HE DID IT, BRAINS! WITH ONE MINUTE TO SPARE!
I-ER-I HAD A HUNCH WE'D MAKE OUT IN THE END, VIRGIL. NOW, IF THE DOORS ARE OPEN, WE'D BETTER MAKE RADIO CONTACT WITH PROJECT CITY AND EXPLAIN...
TROUBLE IS, THOSE GUYS WILL THINK IT'S ALL BEEN ROUTINE. THEY'LL NEVER KNOW JUST HOW CLOSE THEY CAME!

Part 1 - dateline 25 October 2069

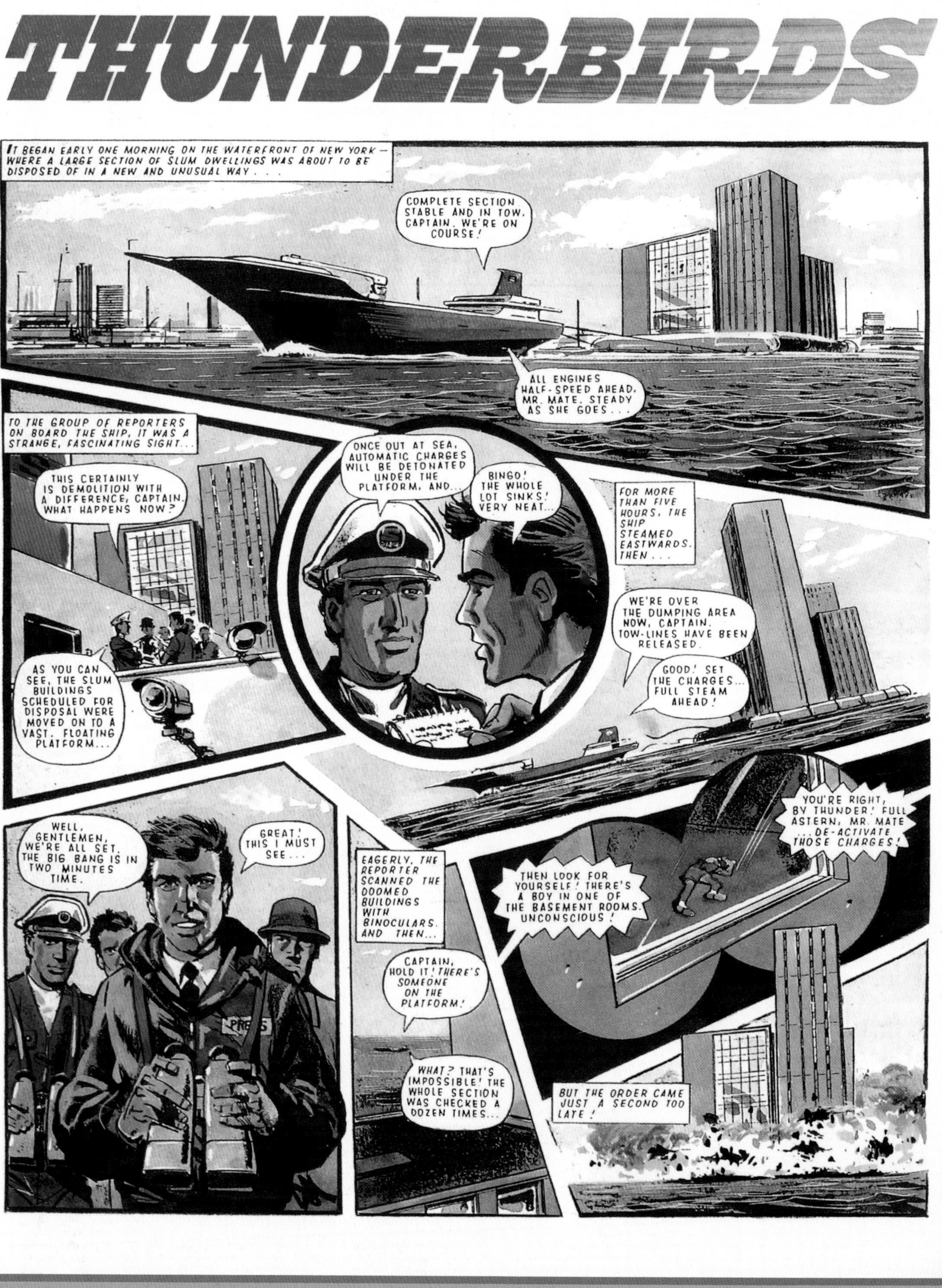
THUNDERBIRDS
IT BEGAN EARLY ONE MORNING ON THE WATERFRONT OF NEW YORK — WHERE A LARGE SECTION OF SLUM DWELLINGS WAS ABOUT TO BE DISPOSED OF IN A NEW AND UNUSUAL WAY . . .
COMPLETE SECTION STABLE AND IN TOW, CAPTAIN. WE'RE ON COURSE!
ALL ENGINES HALF-SPEED AHEAD, MR. MATE. STEADY AS SHE GOES . . .
TO THE GROUP OF REPORTERS ON BOARD THE SHIP, IT WAS A STRANGE, FASCINATING SIGHT...
THIS CERTAINLY IS DEMOLITION WITH A DIFFERENCE, CAPTAIN. WHAT HAPPENS NOW?
AS YOU CAN SEE, THE SLUM BUILDINGS SCHEDULED FOR DISPOSAL WERE MOVED ON TO A VAST, FLOATING PLATFORM...
ONCE OUT AT SEA, AUTOMATIC CHARGES WILL BE DETONATED UNDER THE PLATFORM, AND...
BINGO! THE WHOLE LOT SINKS! VERY NEAT...
FOR MORE THAN FIVE HOURS, THE SHIP STEAMED EASTWARDS. THEN . . .
WE'RE OVER THE DUMPING AREA NOW, CAPTAIN. TOW-LINES HAVE BEEN RELEASED.
GOOD! SET THE CHARGES... FULL STEAM AHEAD!
WELL, GENTLEMEN, WE'RE ALL SET. THE BIG BANG IS IN TWO MINUTES TIME.
GREAT! THIS I MUST SEE...
PRESS
EAGERLY, THE REPORTER SCANNED THE DOOMED BUILDINGS WITH BINOCULARS. AND THEN...
CAPTAIN, HOLD IT! THERE'S SOMEONE ON THE PLATFORM!
WHAT? THAT'S IMPOSSIBLE! THE WHOLE SECTION WAS CHECKED A DOZEN TIMES...
THEN LOOK FOR YOURSELF! THERE'S A BOY IN ONE OF THE BASEMENT ROOMS. UNCONSCIOUS!
YOU'RE RIGHT, BY THUNDER! FULL ASTERN, MR. MATE ... DE-ACTIVATE THOSE CHARGES!
BUT THE ORDER CAME JUST A SECOND TOO LATE!

Artist: John Cooper

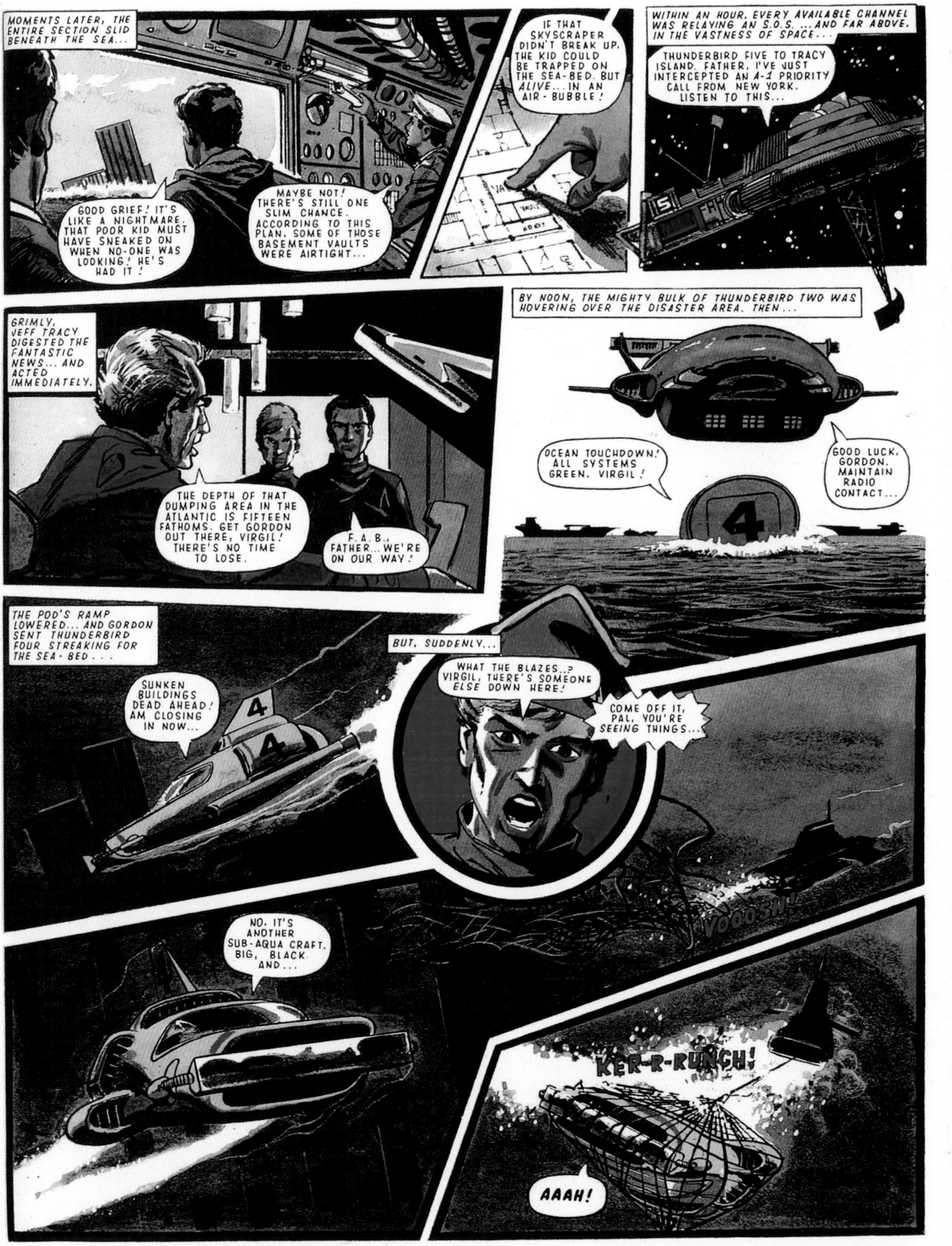

MOMENTS LATER, THE ENTIRE SECTION SLID BENEATH THE SEA...
GOOD GRIEF! IT'S LIKE A NIGHTMARE. THAT POOR KID MUST HAVE SNEAKED ON WHEN NO-ONE WAS LOOKING! HE'S HAD IT!
MAYBE NOT! THERE'S STILL ONE SLIM CHANCE. ACCORDING TO THIS PLAN, SOME OF THOSE BASEMENT VAULTS WERE AIRTIGHT...
IF THAT SKYSCRAPER DIDN'T BREAK UP, THE KID COULD BE TRAPPED ON THE SEA-BED. BUT ALIVE... IN AN AIR-BUBBLE!
WITHIN AN HOUR, EVERY AVAILABLE CHANNEL WAS RELAYING AN S.O.S. ...AND FAR ABOVE, IN THE VASTNESS OF SPACE...
THUNDERBIRD FIVE TO TRACY ISLAND. FATHER, I'VE JUST INTERCEPTED AN A-1 PRIORITY CALL FROM NEW YORK. LISTEN TO THIS...
GRIMLY, JEFF TRACY DIGESTED THE FANTASTIC NEWS... AND ACTED IMMEDIATELY.
THE DEPTH OF THAT DUMPING AREA IN THE ATLANTIC IS FIFTEEN FATHOMS. GET GORDON OUT THERE, VIRGIL! THERE'S NO TIME TO LOSE.
F.A.B., FATHER... WE'RE ON OUR WAY!
BY NOON, THE MIGHTY BULK OF THUNDERBIRD TWO WAS HOVERING OVER THE DISASTER AREA. THEN...
OCEAN TOUCHDOWN! ALL SYSTEMS GREEN, VIRGIL!
GOOD LUCK, GORDON. MAINTAIN RADIO CONTACT...
THE POD'S RAMP LOWERED... AND GORDON SENT THUNDERBIRD FOUR STREAKING FOR THE SEA-BED...
SUNKEN BUILDINGS DEAD AHEAD! AM CLOSING IN NOW...
BUT, SUDDENLY...
WHAT THE BLAZES..? VIRGIL, THERE'S SOMEONE ELSE DOWN HERE!
COME OFF IT, PAL, YOU'RE SEEING THINGS...
VOOOSH!
NO, IT'S ANOTHER SUB-AQUA CRAFT. BIG, BLACK AND...
KER-R-RUNCH!
AAAH!

Part 2 - dateline 01 November 2069

THUNDERBIRDS

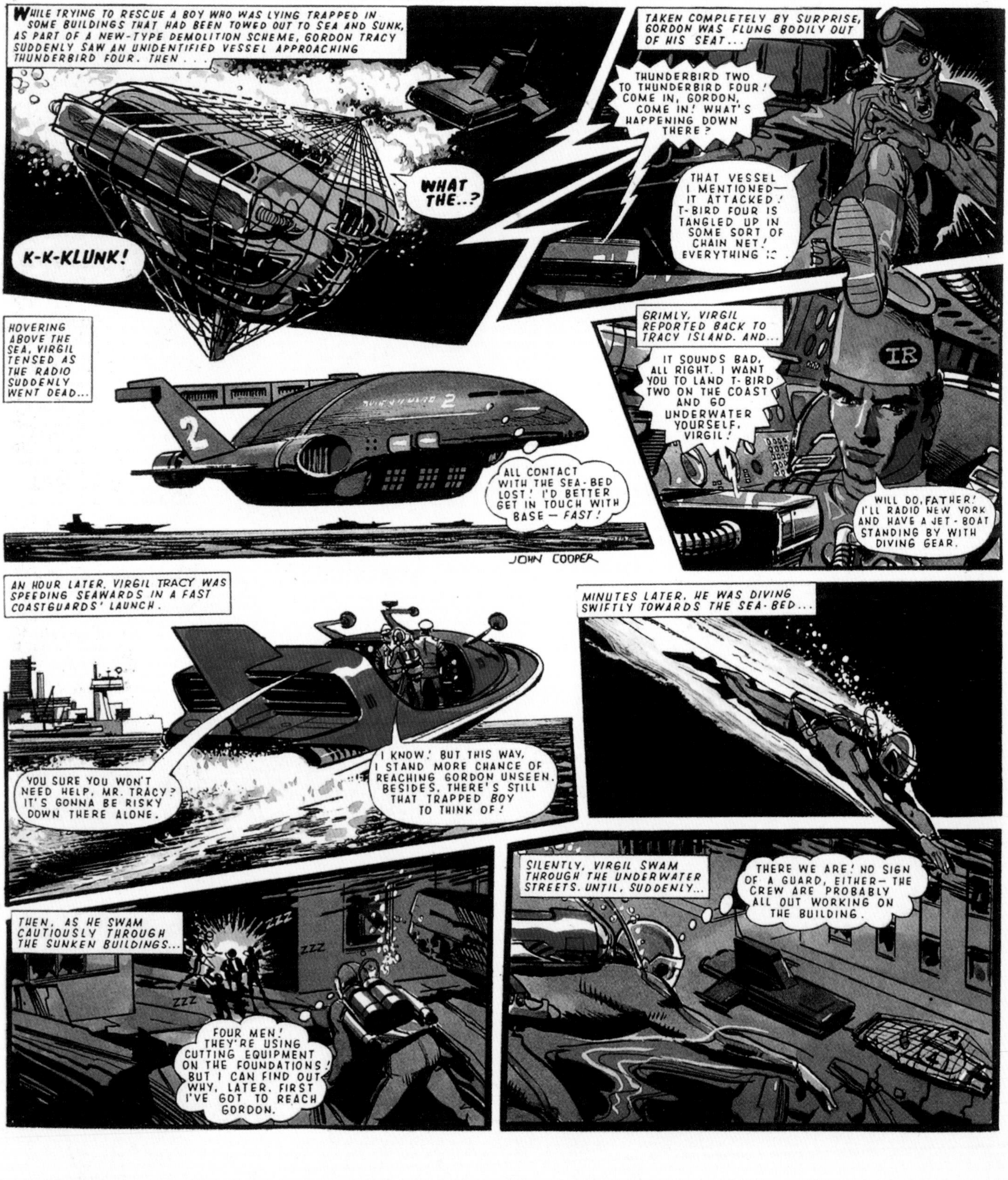
WHILE TRYING TO RESCUE A BOY WHO WAS LYING TRAPPED IN SOME BUILDINGS THAT HAD BEEN TOWED OUT TO SEA AND SUNK, AS PART OF A NEW-TYPE DEMOLITION SCHEME, GORDON TRACY SUDDENLY SAW AN UNIDENTIFIED VESSEL APPROACHING THUNDERBIRD FOUR. THEN . . .
WHAT THE..?
K-K-KLUNK!
TAKEN COMPLETELY BY SURPRISE, GORDON WAS FLUNG BODILY OUT OF HIS SEAT...
THUNDERBIRD TWO TO THUNDERBIRD FOUR! COME IN, GORDON, COME IN! WHAT'S HAPPENING DOWN THERE?
THAT VESSEL I MENTIONED— IT ATTACKED! T-BIRD FOUR IS TANGLED UP IN SOME SORT OF CHAIN NET! EVERYTHING
HOVERING ABOVE THE SEA, VIRGIL TENSED AS THE RADIO SUDDENLY WENT DEAD...
2
ALL CONTACT WITH THE SEA-BED LOST! I'D BETTER GET IN TOUCH WITH BASE — FAST!
JOHN COOPER
GRIMLY, VIRGIL REPORTED BACK TO TRACY ISLAND. AND...
IT SOUNDS BAD, ALL RIGHT. I WANT YOU TO LAND T-BIRD TWO ON THE COAST AND GO UNDERWATER YOURSELF, VIRGIL!
IR
WILL DO, FATHER! I'LL RADIO NEW YORK AND HAVE A JET-BOAT STANDING BY WITH DIVING GEAR.
AN HOUR LATER, VIRGIL TRACY WAS SPEEDING SEAWARDS IN A FAST COASTGUARDS' LAUNCH.
YOU SURE YOU WON'T NEED HELP, MR. TRACY? IT'S GONNA BE RISKY DOWN THERE ALONE.
I KNOW! BUT THIS WAY, I STAND MORE CHANCE OF REACHING GORDON UNSEEN. BESIDES, THERE'S STILL THAT TRAPPED BOY TO THINK OF!
MINUTES LATER, HE WAS DIVING SWIFTLY TOWARDS THE SEA-BED...
THEN, AS HE SWAM CAUTIOUSLY THROUGH THE SUNKEN BUILDINGS...
ZZZ
ZZZ
ZZZ
FOUR MEN! THEY'RE USING CUTTING EQUIPMENT ON THE FOUNDATIONS! BUT I CAN FIND OUT WHY, LATER. FIRST I'VE GOT TO REACH GORDON.
SILENTLY, VIRGIL SWAM THROUGH THE UNDERWATER STREETS. UNTIL, SUDDENLY...
THERE WE ARE! NO SIGN OF A GUARD, EITHER— THE CREW ARE PROBABLY ALL OUT WORKING ON THE BUILDING.

Artist: John Cooper

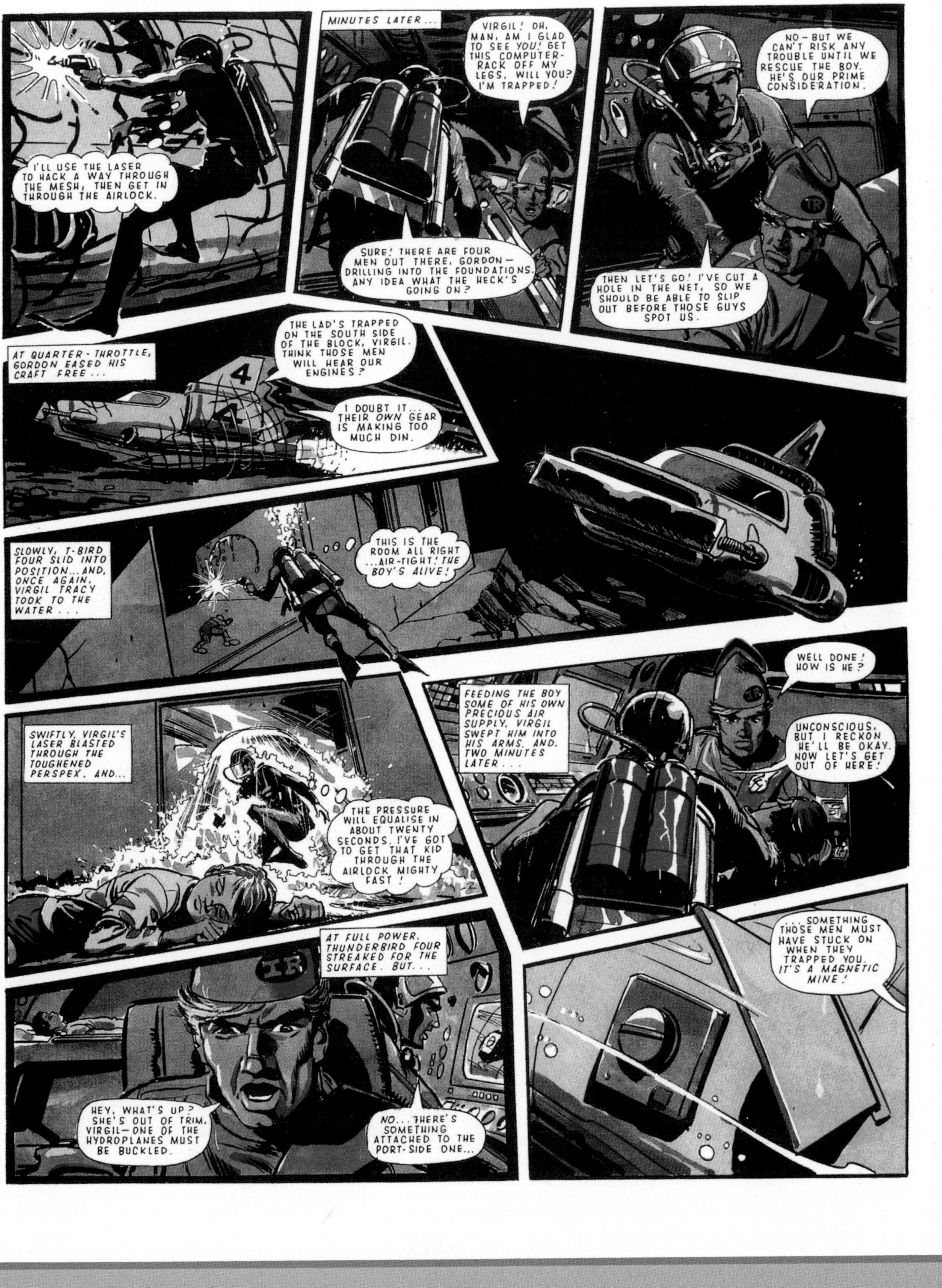
I'LL USE THE LASER TO HACK A WAY THROUGH THE MESH, THEN GET IN THROUGH THE AIRLOCK.
MINUTES LATER...
VIRGIL! OH, MAN, AM I GLAD TO SEE YOU! GET THIS COMPUTER-RACK OFF MY LEGS, WILL YOU? I'M TRAPPED!
SURE! THERE ARE FOUR MEN OUT THERE, GORDON— DRILLING INTO THE FOUNDATIONS. ANY IDEA WHAT THE HECK'S GOING ON?
NO—BUT WE CAN'T RISK ANY TROUBLE UNTIL WE RESCUE THE BOY. HE'S OUR PRIME CONSIDERATION.
THEN LET'S GO! I'VE CUT A HOLE IN THE NET, SO WE SHOULD BE ABLE TO SLIP OUT BEFORE THOSE GUYS SPOT US.
AT QUARTER-THROTTLE, GORDON EASED HIS CRAFT FREE...
THE LAD'S TRAPPED ON THE SOUTH SIDE OF THE BLOCK, VIRGIL. THINK THOSE MEN WILL HEAR OUR ENGINES?
I DOUBT IT... THEIR OWN GEAR IS MAKING TOO MUCH DIN.
SLOWLY, T-BIRD FOUR SLID INTO POSITION...AND, ONCE AGAIN, VIRGIL TRACY TOOK TO THE WATER...
THIS IS THE ROOM ALL RIGHT ...AIR-TIGHT! THE BOY'S ALIVE!
SWIFTLY, VIRGIL'S LASER BLASTED THROUGH THE TOUGHENED PERSPEX. AND...
THE PRESSURE WILL EQUALISE IN ABOUT TWENTY SECONDS. I'VE GOT TO GET THAT KID THROUGH THE AIRLOCK MIGHTY FAST!
FEEDING THE BOY SOME OF HIS OWN PRECIOUS AIR SUPPLY, VIRGIL SWEPT HIM INTO HIS ARMS. AND, TWO MINUTES LATER...
WELL DONE! HOW IS HE?
UNCONSCIOUS, BUT I RECKON HE'LL BE OKAY. NOW LET'S GET OUT OF HERE!
AT FULL POWER, THUNDERBIRD FOUR STREAKED FOR THE SURFACE. BUT...
HEY, WHAT'S UP? SHE'S OUT OF TRIM, VIRGIL—ONE OF THE HYDROPLANES MUST BE BUCKLED.
NO...THERE'S SOMETHING ATTACHED TO THE PORT-SIDE ONE...
...SOMETHING THOSE MEN MUST HAVE STUCK ON WHEN THEY TRAPPED YOU. IT'S A MAGNETIC MINE!

Part 3 - dateline 08 November 2069

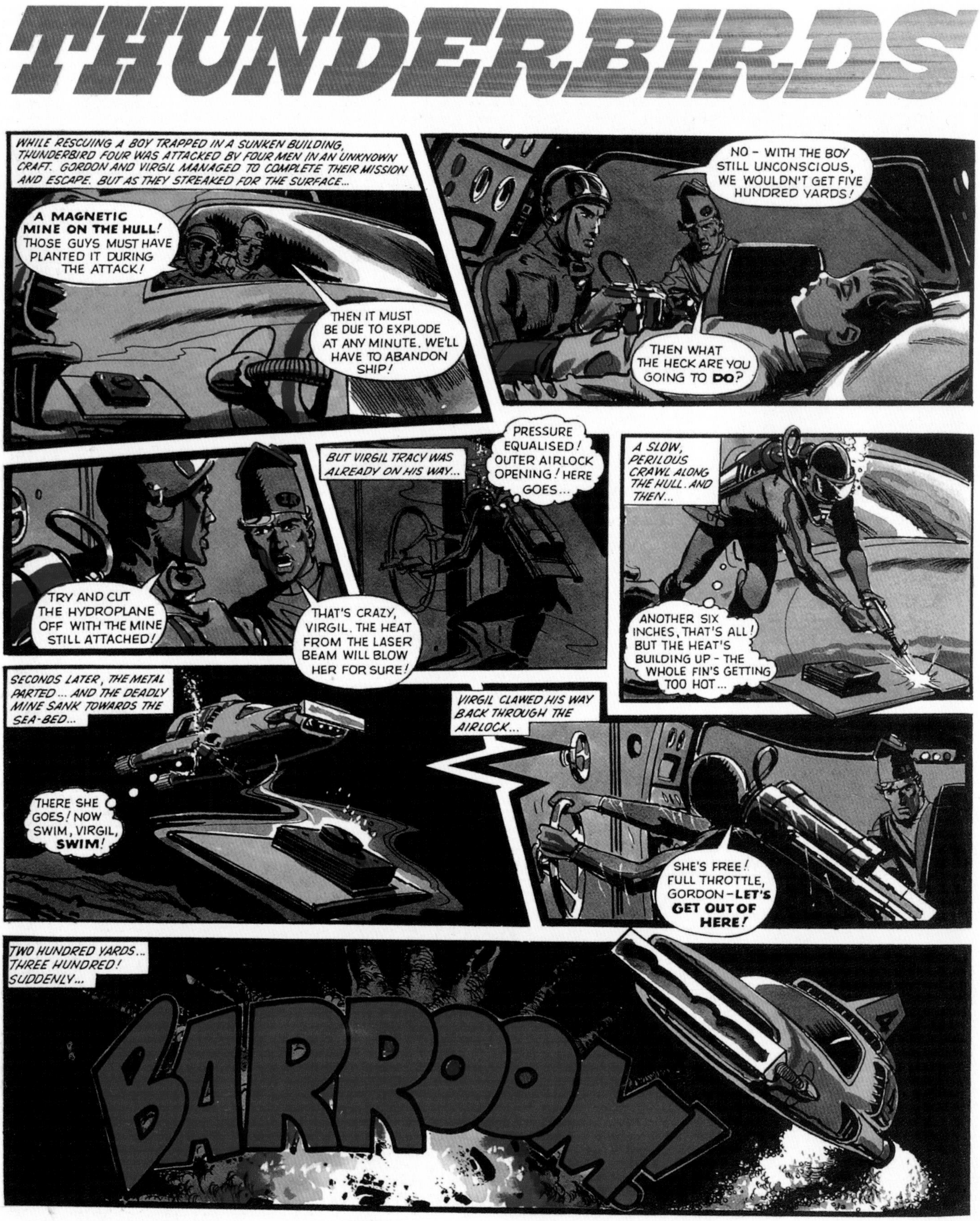
THUNDERBIRDS
WHILE RESCUING A BOY TRAPPED IN A SUNKEN BUILDING, THUNDERBIRD FOUR WAS ATTACKED BY FOUR MEN IN AN UNKNOWN CRAFT. GORDON AND VIRGIL MANAGED TO COMPLETE THEIR MISSION AND ESCAPE. BUT AS THEY STREAKED FOR THE SURFACE...
A MAGNETIC MINE ON THE HULL! THOSE GUYS MUST HAVE PLANTED IT DURING THE ATTACK!
THEN IT MUST BE DUE TO EXPLODE AT ANY MINUTE. WE'LL HAVE TO ABANDON SHIP!
NO - WITH THE BOY STILL UNCONSCIOUS, WE WOULDN'T GET FIVE HUNDRED YARDS!
THEN WHAT THE HECK ARE YOU GOING TO DO?
TRY AND CUT THE HYDROPLANE OFF WITH THE MINE STILL ATTACHED!
THAT'S CRAZY, VIRGIL. THE HEAT FROM THE LASER BEAM WILL BLOW HER FOR SURE!
BUT VIRGIL TRACY WAS ALREADY ON HIS WAY...
PRESSURE EQUALISED! OUTER AIRLOCK OPENING! HERE GOES...
A SLOW, PERILOUS CRAWL ALONG THE HULL. AND THEN...
ANOTHER SIX INCHES, THAT'S ALL! BUT THE HEAT'S BUILDING UP - THE WHOLE FIN'S GETTING TOO HOT...
SECONDS LATER, THE METAL PARTED ... AND THE DEADLY MINE SANK TOWARDS THE SEA-BED...
THERE SHE GOES! NOW SWIM, VIRGIL, SWIM!
VIRGIL CLAWED HIS WAY BACK THROUGH THE AIRLOCK...
SHE'S FREE! FULL THROTTLE, GORDON - LET'S GET OUT OF HERE!
TWO HUNDRED YARDS... THREE HUNDRED! SUDDENLY...
BARROOM!

Artist: John Cooper

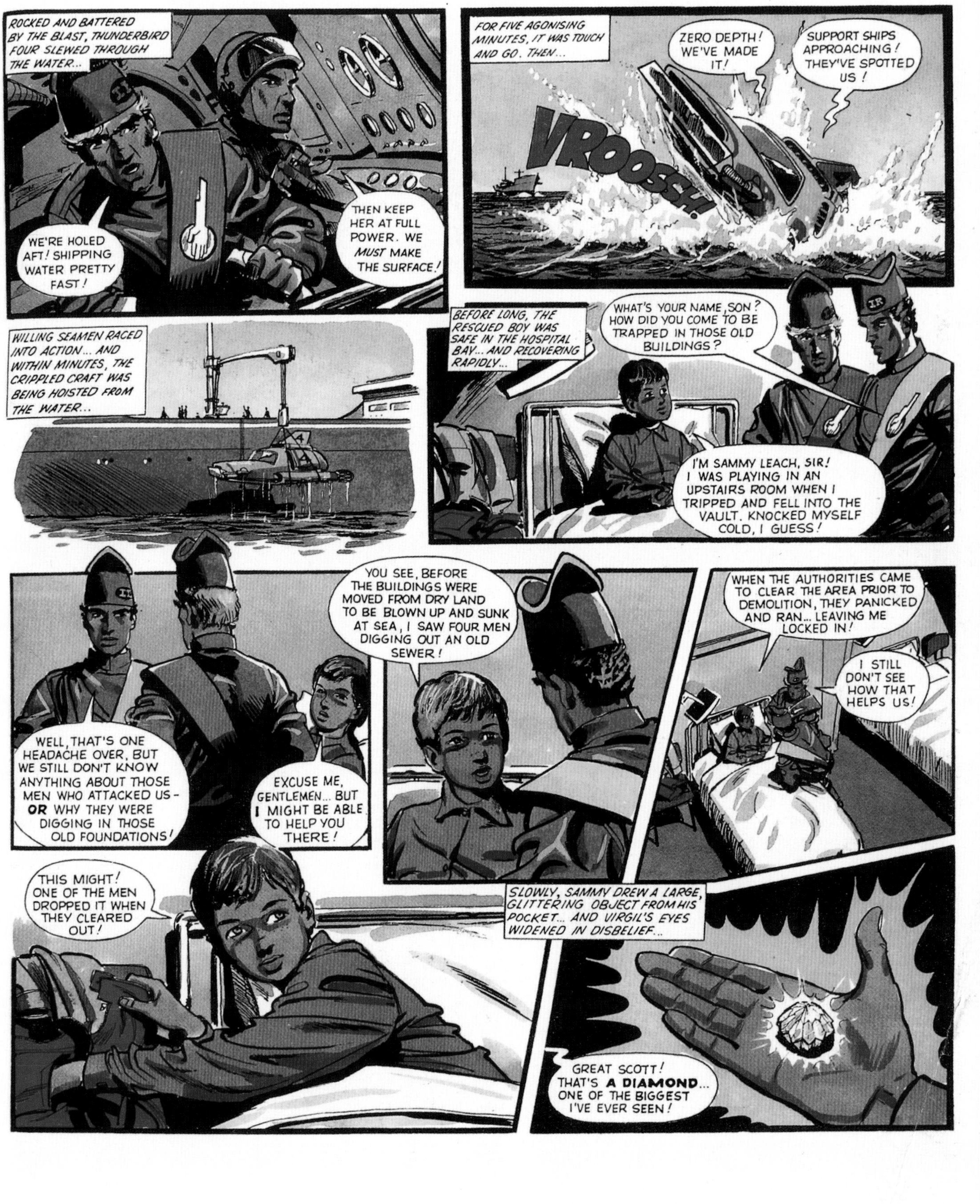
ROCKED AND BATTERED BY THE BLAST, THUNDERBIRD FOUR SLEWED THROUGH THE WATER...
WE'RE HOLED AFT! SHIPPING WATER PRETTY FAST!
THEN KEEP HER AT FULL POWER. WE MUST MAKE THE SURFACE!
FOR FIVE AGONISING MINUTES, IT WAS TOUCH AND GO. THEN...
ZERO DEPTH! WE'VE MADE IT!
SUPPORT SHIPS APPROACHING! THEY'VE SPOTTED US!
VROOSSH!
WILLING SEAMEN RACED INTO ACTION... AND WITHIN MINUTES, THE CRIPPLED CRAFT WAS BEING HOISTED FROM THE WATER...
BEFORE LONG, THE RESCUED BOY WAS SAFE IN THE HOSPITAL BAY... AND RECOVERING RAPIDLY...
WHAT'S YOUR NAME, SON? HOW DID YOU COME TO BE TRAPPED IN THOSE OLD BUILDINGS?
I'M SAMMY LEACH, SIR! I WAS PLAYING IN AN UPSTAIRS ROOM WHEN I TRIPPED AND FELL INTO THE VAULT. KNOCKED MYSELF COLD, I GUESS!
WELL, THAT'S ONE HEADACHE OVER, BUT WE STILL DON'T KNOW ANYTHING ABOUT THOSE MEN WHO ATTACKED US - OR WHY THEY WERE DIGGING IN THOSE OLD FOUNDATIONS!
EXCUSE ME, GENTLEMEN... BUT I MIGHT BE ABLE TO HELP YOU THERE!
YOU SEE, BEFORE THE BUILDINGS WERE MOVED FROM DRY LAND TO BE BLOWN UP AND SUNK AT SEA, I SAW FOUR MEN DIGGING OUT AN OLD SEWER!
WHEN THE AUTHORITIES CAME TO CLEAR THE AREA PRIOR TO DEMOLITION, THEY PANICKED AND RAN... LEAVING ME LOCKED IN!
I STILL DON'T SEE HOW THAT HELPS US!
THIS MIGHT! ONE OF THE MEN DROPPED IT WHEN THEY CLEARED OUT!
SLOWLY, SAMMY DREW A LARGE, GLITTERING OBJECT FROM HIS POCKET... AND VIRGIL'S EYES WIDENED IN DISBELIEF...
GREAT SCOTT! THAT'S A DIAMOND... ONE OF THE BIGGEST I'VE EVER SEEN!

Part 4 - dateline 15 November 2069

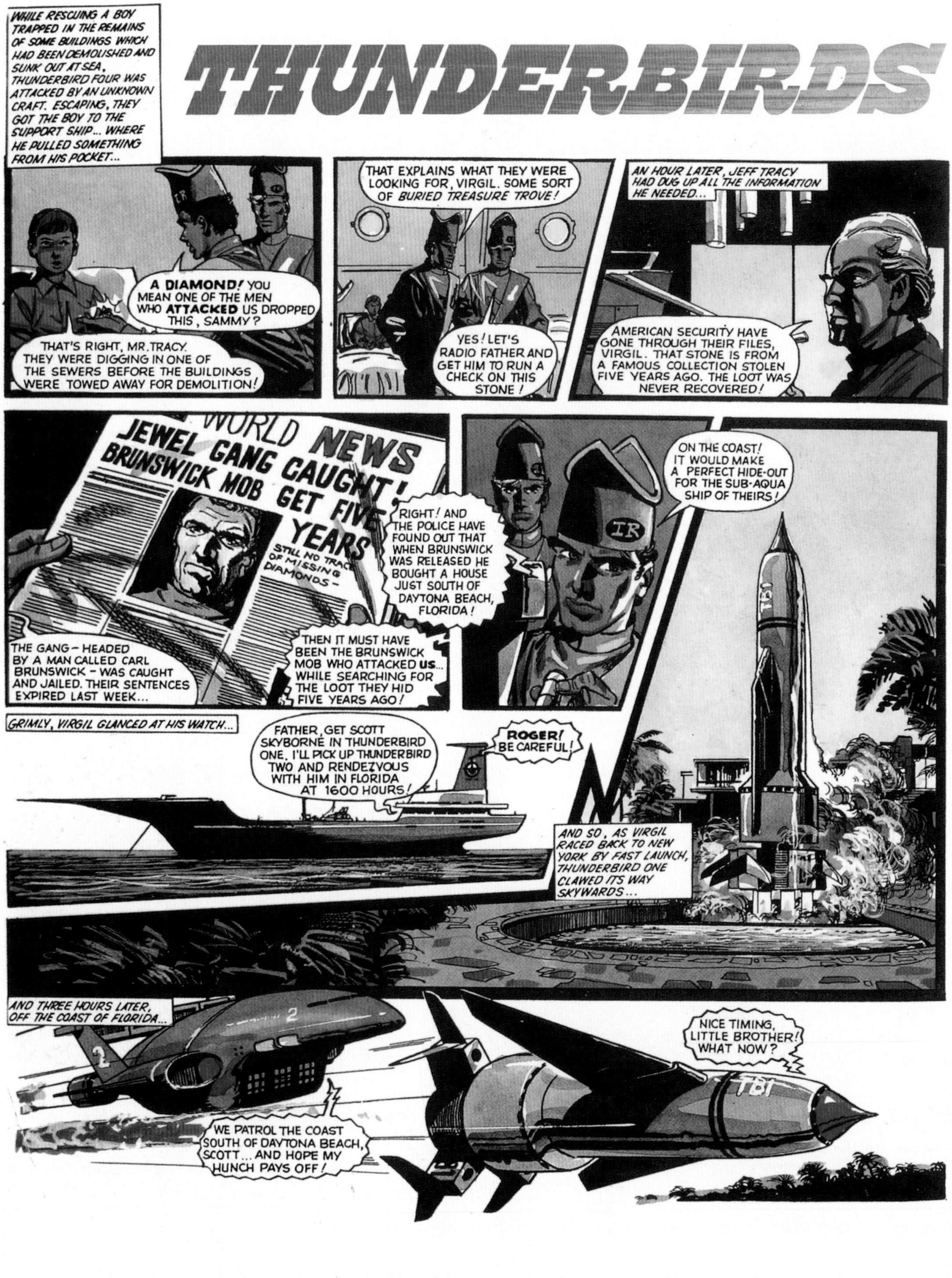
WHILE RESCUING A BOY TRAPPED IN THE REMAINS OF SOME BUILDINGS WHICH HAD BEEN DEMOLISHED AND SUNK OUT AT SEA, THUNDERBIRD FOUR WAS ATTACKED BY AN UNKNOWN CRAFT. ESCAPING, THEY GOT THE BOY TO THE SUPPORT SHIP... WHERE HE PULLED SOMETHING FROM HIS POCKET...
THUNDERBIRDS
A DIAMOND! YOU MEAN ONE OF THE MEN WHO ATTACKED US DROPPED THIS, SAMMY?
THAT'S RIGHT, MR. TRACY. THEY WERE DIGGING IN ONE OF THE SEWERS BEFORE THE BUILDINGS WERE TOWED AWAY FOR DEMOLITION!
THAT EXPLAINS WHAT THEY WERE LOOKING FOR, VIRGIL. SOME SORT OF BURIED TREASURE TROVE!
YES! LET'S RADIO FATHER AND GET HIM TO RUN A CHECK ON THIS STONE!
AN HOUR LATER, JEFF TRACY HAD DUG UP ALL THE INFORMATION HE NEEDED...
AMERICAN SECURITY HAVE GONE THROUGH THEIR FILES, VIRGIL. THAT STONE IS FROM A FAMOUS COLLECTION STOLEN FIVE YEARS AGO. THE LOOT WAS NEVER RECOVERED!
WORLD NEWS
JEWEL GANG CAUGHT!
BRUNSWICK MOB GET FIVE YEARS
STILL NO TRACE OF MISSING DIAMONDS -
THE GANG - HEADED BY A MAN CALLED CARL BRUNSWICK - WAS CAUGHT AND JAILED. THEIR SENTENCES EXPIRED LAST WEEK...
THEN IT MUST HAVE BEEN THE BRUNSWICK MOB WHO ATTACKED US... WHILE SEARCHING FOR THE LOOT THEY HID FIVE YEARS AGO!
RIGHT! AND THE POLICE HAVE FOUND OUT THAT WHEN BRUNSWICK WAS RELEASED HE BOUGHT A HOUSE JUST SOUTH OF DAYTONA BEACH, FLORIDA!
ON THE COAST! IT WOULD MAKE A PERFECT HIDE-OUT FOR THE SUB-AQUA SHIP OF THEIRS!
GRIMLY, VIRGIL GLANCED AT HIS WATCH...
FATHER, GET SCOTT SKYBORNE IN THUNDERBIRD ONE. I'LL PICK UP THUNDERBIRD TWO AND RENDEZVOUS WITH HIM IN FLORIDA AT 1600 HOURS!
ROGER! BE CAREFUL!
AND SO, AS VIRGIL RACED BACK TO NEW YORK BY FAST LAUNCH, THUNDERBIRD ONE CLAWED ITS WAY SKYWARDS...
AND THREE HOURS LATER, OFF THE COAST OF FLORIDA...
NICE TIMING, LITTLE BROTHER! WHAT NOW?
WE PATROL THE COAST SOUTH OF DAYTONA BEACH, SCOTT... AND HOPE MY HUNCH PAYS OFF!

Artist: John Cooper

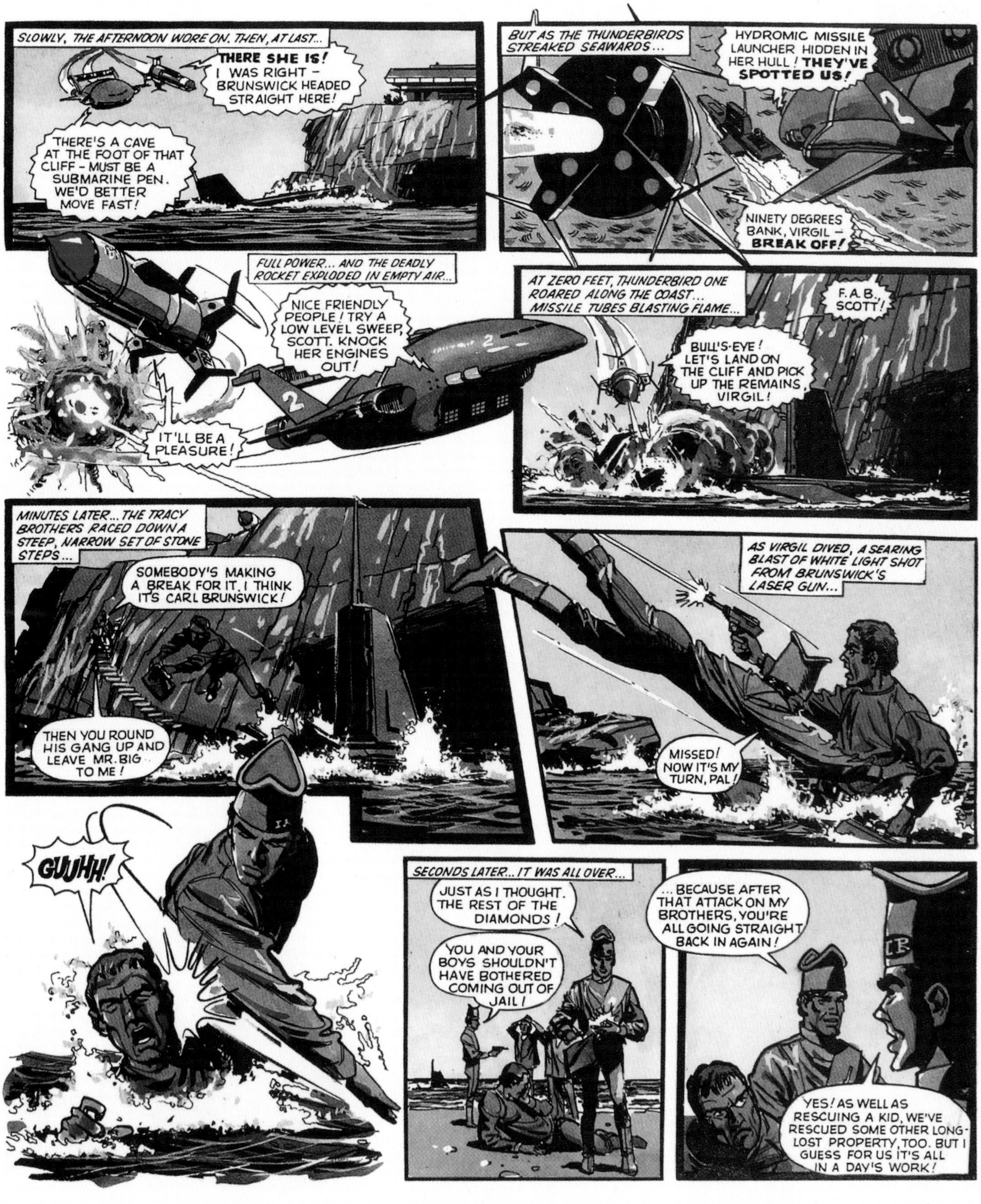
SLOWLY, THE AFTERNOON WORE ON. THEN, AT LAST...
THERE SHE IS! I WAS RIGHT – BRUNSWICK HEADED STRAIGHT HERE!
THERE'S A CAVE AT THE FOOT OF THAT CLIFF – MUST BE A SUBMARINE PEN. WE'D BETTER MOVE FAST!
BUT AS THE THUNDERBIRDS STREAKED SEAWARDS...
HYDROMIC MISSILE LAUNCHER HIDDEN IN HER HULL! THEY'VE SPOTTED US!
NINETY DEGREES BANK, VIRGIL – BREAK OFF!
FULL POWER... AND THE DEADLY ROCKET EXPLODED IN EMPTY AIR...
NICE FRIENDLY PEOPLE! TRY A LOW LEVEL SWEEP, SCOTT. KNOCK HER ENGINES OUT!
IT'LL BE A PLEASURE!
AT ZERO FEET, THUNDERBIRD ONE ROARED ALONG THE COAST... MISSILE TUBES BLASTING FLAME...
F.A.B., SCOTT!
BULL'S-EYE! LET'S LAND ON THE CLIFF AND PICK UP THE REMAINS, VIRGIL!
MINUTES LATER... THE TRACY BROTHERS RACED DOWN A STEEP, NARROW SET OF STONE STEPS...
SOMEBODY'S MAKING A BREAK FOR IT. I THINK ITS CARL BRUNSWICK!
THEN YOU ROUND HIS GANG UP AND LEAVE MR. BIG TO ME!
AS VIRGIL DIVED, A SEARING BLAST OF WHITE LIGHT SHOT FROM BRUNSWICK'S LASER GUN...
MISSED! NOW IT'S MY TURN, PAL!
GUUHH!
SECONDS LATER... IT WAS ALL OVER...
JUST AS I THOUGHT. THE REST OF THE DIAMONDS!
YOU AND YOUR BOYS SHOULDN'T HAVE BOTHERED COMING OUT OF JAIL!
...BECAUSE AFTER THAT ATTACK ON MY BROTHERS, YOU'RE ALL GOING STRAIGHT BACK IN AGAIN!
YES! AS WELL AS RESCUING A KID, WE'VE RESCUED SOME OTHER LONG-LOST PROPERTY, TOO. BUT I GUESS FOR US IT'S ALL IN A DAY'S WORK!

Part 1 - dateline 21 February 2070

THUNDERBIRDS

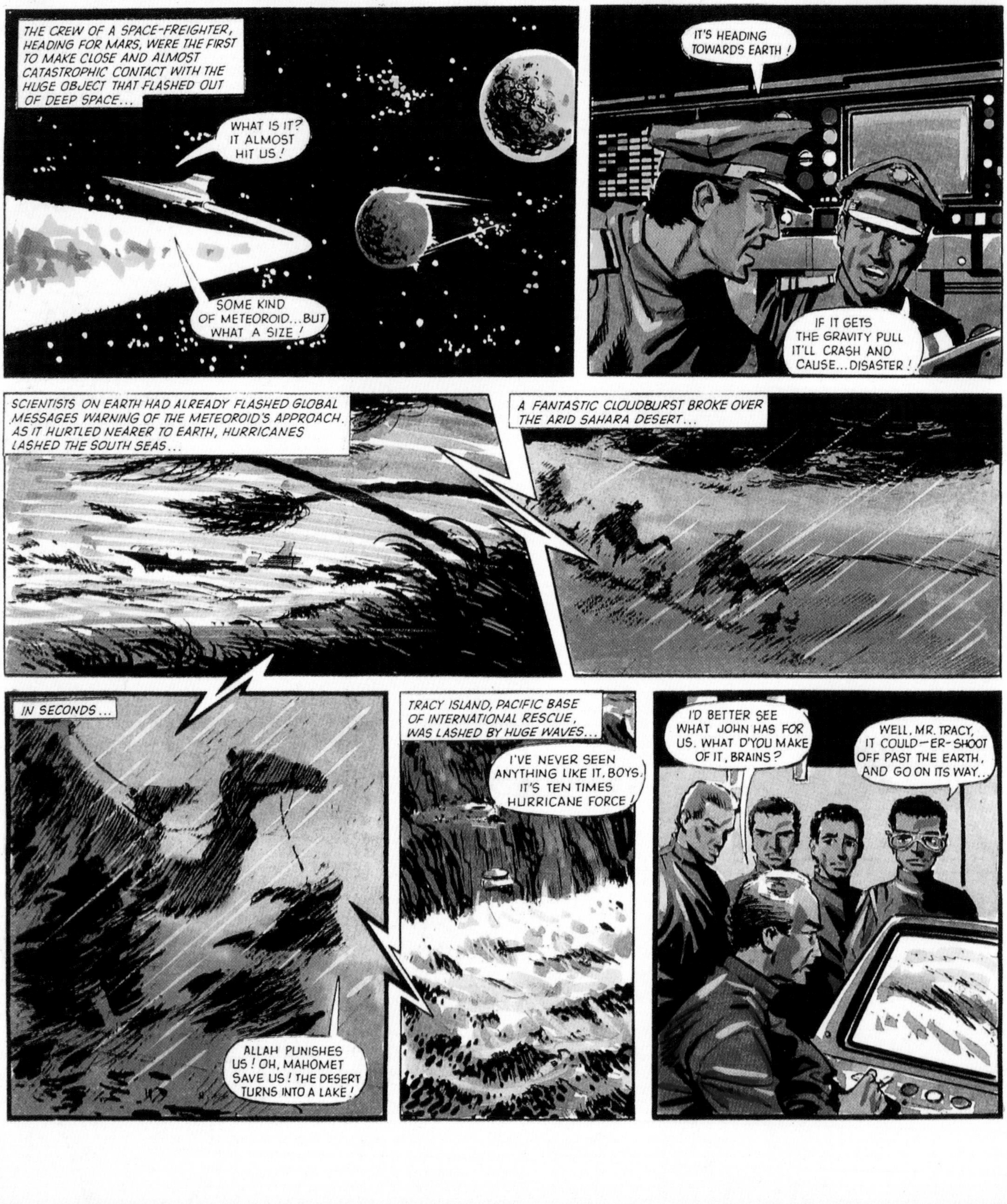
THE CREW OF A SPACE-FREIGHTER, HEADING FOR MARS, WERE THE FIRST TO MAKE CLOSE AND ALMOST CATASTROPHIC CONTACT WITH THE HUGE OBJECT THAT FLASHED OUT OF DEEP SPACE...
WHAT IS IT? IT ALMOST HIT US!
SOME KIND OF METEOROID... BUT WHAT A SIZE!
IT'S HEADING TOWARDS EARTH!
IF IT GETS THE GRAVITY PULL IT'LL CRASH AND CAUSE... DISASTER!
SCIENTISTS ON EARTH HAD ALREADY FLASHED GLOBAL MESSAGES WARNING OF THE METEOROID'S APPROACH. AS IT HURTLED NEARER TO EARTH, HURRICANES LASHED THE SOUTH SEAS...
A FANTASTIC CLOUDBURST BROKE OVER THE ARID SAHARA DESERT...
IN SECONDS...
ALLAH PUNISHES US! OH, MAHOMET SAVE US! THE DESERT TURNS INTO A LAKE!
TRACY ISLAND, PACIFIC BASE OF INTERNATIONAL RESCUE, WAS LASHED BY HUGE WAVES...
I'VE NEVER SEEN ANYTHING LIKE IT, BOYS. IT'S TEN TIMES HURRICANE FORCE!
I'D BETTER SEE WHAT JOHN HAS FOR US. WHAT D'YOU MAKE OF IT, BRAINS?
WELL, MR. TRACY, IT COULD—ER-SHOOT OFF PAST THE EARTH, AND GO ON ITS WAY...

Artist: John Cooper

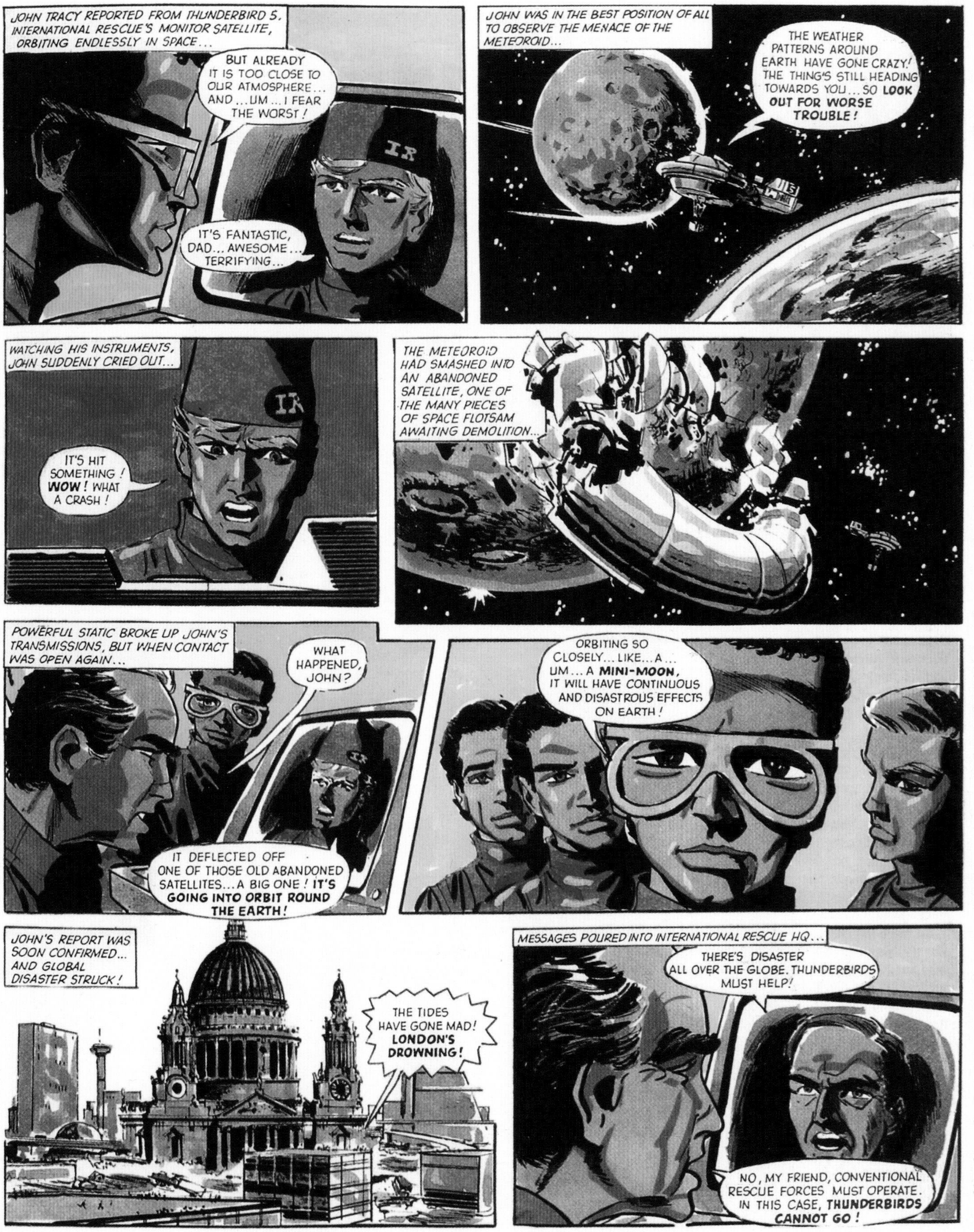
JOHN TRACY REPORTED FROM THUNDERBIRD 5, INTERNATIONAL RESCUE'S MONITOR SATELLITE, ORBITING ENDLESSLY IN SPACE...
BUT ALREADY IT IS TOO CLOSE TO OUR ATMOSPHERE... AND... UM... I FEAR THE WORST!
IT'S FANTASTIC, DAD... AWESOME... TERRIFYING...
JOHN WAS IN THE BEST POSITION OF ALL TO OBSERVE THE MENACE OF THE METEOROID...
THE WEATHER PATTERNS AROUND EARTH HAVE GONE CRAZY! THE THING'S STILL HEADING TOWARDS YOU... SO LOOK OUT FOR WORSE TROUBLE!
WATCHING HIS INSTRUMENTS, JOHN SUDDENLY CRIED OUT...
IT'S HIT SOMETHING! WOW! WHAT A CRASH!
THE METEOROID HAD SMASHED INTO AN ABANDONED SATELLITE, ONE OF THE MANY PIECES OF SPACE FLOTSAM AWAITING DEMOLITION...
POWERFUL STATIC BROKE UP JOHN'S TRANSMISSIONS, BUT WHEN CONTACT WAS OPEN AGAIN...
WHAT HAPPENED, JOHN?
IT DEFLECTED OFF ONE OF THOSE OLD ABANDONED SATELLITES... A BIG ONE! IT'S GOING INTO ORBIT ROUND THE EARTH!
ORBITING SO CLOSELY... LIKE... A... UM... A MINI-MOON, IT WILL HAVE CONTINUOUS AND DISASTROUS EFFECTS ON EARTH!
JOHN'S REPORT WAS SOON CONFIRMED... AND GLOBAL DISASTER STRUCK!
THE TIDES HAVE GONE MAD! LONDON'S DROWNING!
MESSAGES POURED INTO INTERNATIONAL RESCUE HQ...
THERE'S DISASTER ALL OVER THE GLOBE. THUNDERBIRDS MUST HELP!
NO, MY FRIEND, CONVENTIONAL RESCUE FORCES MUST OPERATE. IN THIS CASE, THUNDERBIRDS CANNOT GO!

Part 2 - dateline 28 February 2070

THUNDERBIRDS

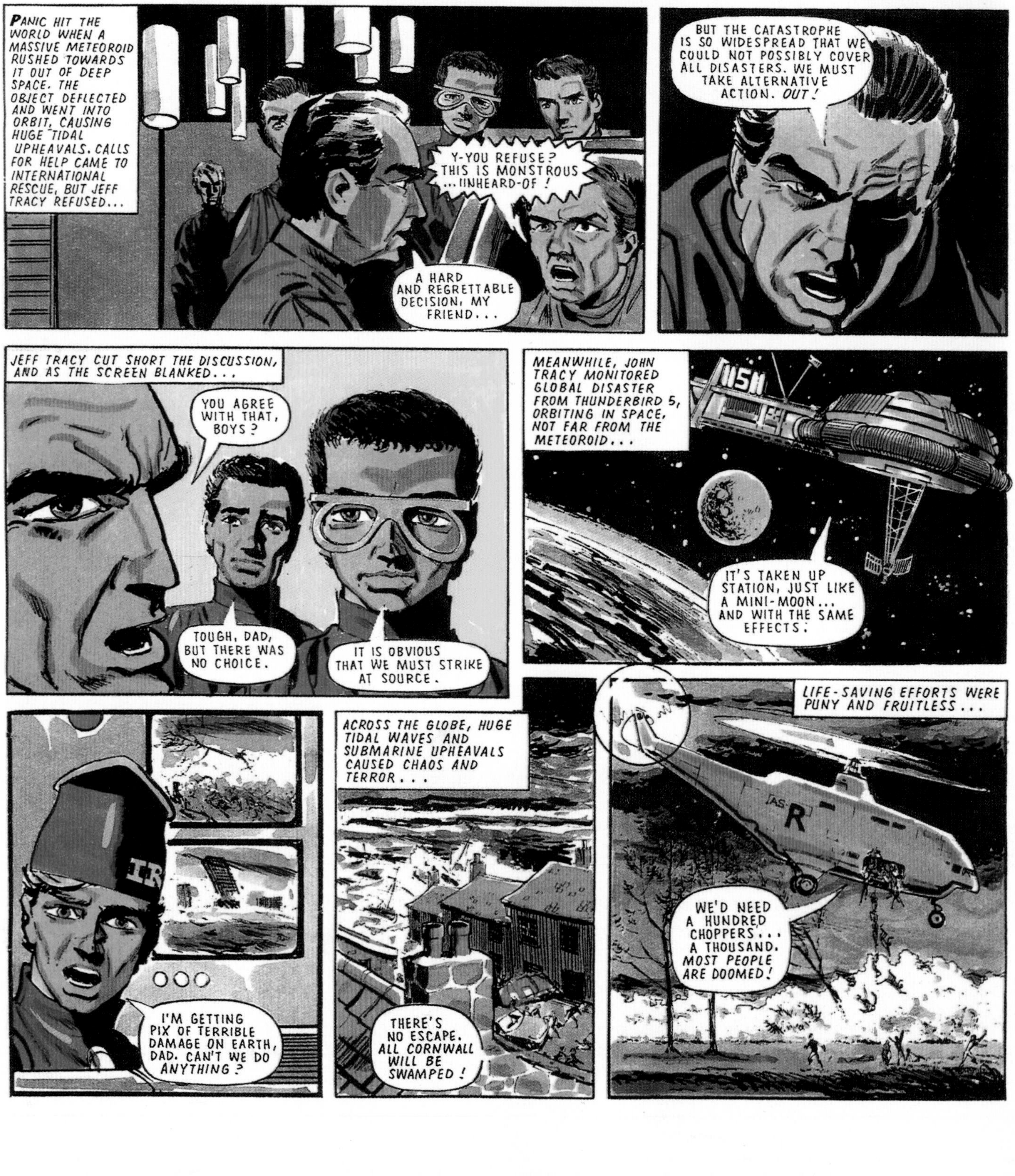
PANIC HIT THE WORLD WHEN A MASSIVE METEOROID RUSHED TOWARDS IT OUT OF DEEP SPACE. THE OBJECT DEFLECTED AND WENT INTO ORBIT, CAUSING HUGE TIDAL UPHEAVALS. CALLS FOR HELP CAME TO INTERNATIONAL RESCUE, BUT JEFF TRACY REFUSED...
Y-YOU REFUSE? THIS IS MONSTROUS ...UNHEARD-OF!
A HARD AND REGRETTABLE DECISION, MY FRIEND...
BUT THE CATASTROPHE IS SO WIDESPREAD THAT WE COULD NOT POSSIBLY COVER ALL DISASTERS. WE MUST TAKE ALTERNATIVE ACTION. OUT!
JEFF TRACY CUT SHORT THE DISCUSSION, AND AS THE SCREEN BLANKED...
YOU AGREE WITH THAT, BOYS?
TOUGH, DAD, BUT THERE WAS NO CHOICE.
IT IS OBVIOUS THAT WE MUST STRIKE AT SOURCE.
MEANWHILE, JOHN TRACY MONITORED GLOBAL DISASTER FROM THUNDERBIRD 5, ORBITING IN SPACE, NOT FAR FROM THE METEOROID...
IT'S TAKEN UP STATION, JUST LIKE A MINI-MOON... AND WITH THE SAME EFFECTS!
I'M GETTING PIX OF TERRIBLE DAMAGE ON EARTH, DAD. CAN'T WE DO ANYTHING?
ACROSS THE GLOBE, HUGE TIDAL WAVES AND SUBMARINE UPHEAVALS CAUSED CHAOS AND TERROR...
THERE'S NO ESCAPE. ALL CORNWALL WILL BE SWAMPED!
LIFE-SAVING EFFORTS WERE PUNY AND FRUITLESS...
WE'D NEED A HUNDRED CHOPPERS... A THOUSAND. MOST PEOPLE ARE DOOMED!

Artist: John Cooper

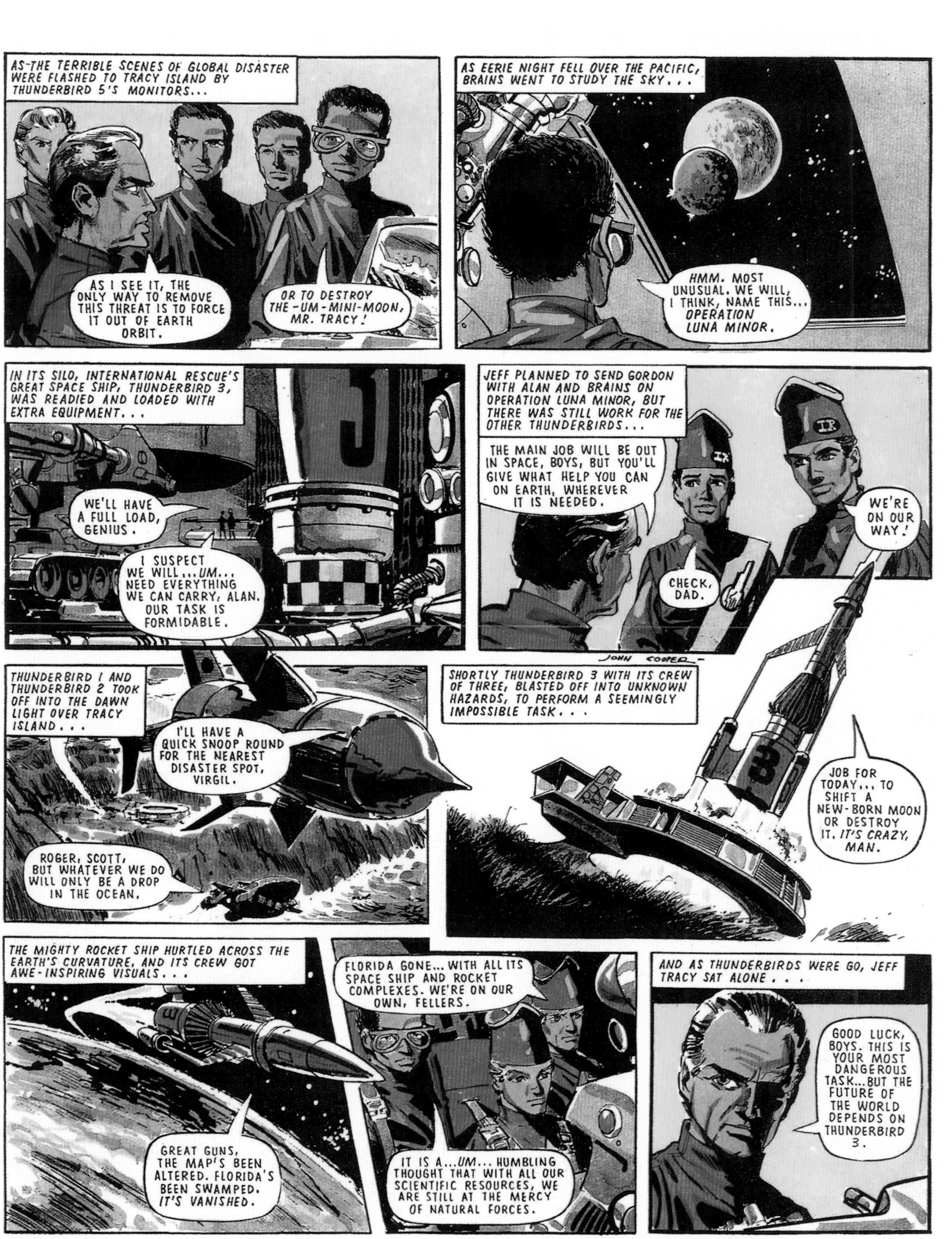
AS THE TERRIBLE SCENES OF GLOBAL DISASTER WERE FLASHED TO TRACY ISLAND BY THUNDERBIRD 5'S MONITORS...
AS I SEE IT, THE ONLY WAY TO REMOVE THIS THREAT IS TO FORCE IT OUT OF EARTH ORBIT.
OR TO DESTROY THE -UM- MINI-MOON, MR. TRACY!
AS EERIE NIGHT FELL OVER THE PACIFIC, BRAINS WENT TO STUDY THE SKY . . .
HMM. MOST UNUSUAL. WE WILL, I THINK, NAME THIS... OPERATION LUNA MINOR.
IN ITS SILO, INTERNATIONAL RESCUE'S GREAT SPACE SHIP, THUNDERBIRD 3, WAS READIED AND LOADED WITH EXTRA EQUIPMENT . . .
WE'LL HAVE A FULL LOAD, GENIUS.
I SUSPECT WE WILL...UM... NEED EVERYTHING WE CAN CARRY, ALAN. OUR TASK IS FORMIDABLE.
JEFF PLANNED TO SEND GORDON WITH ALAN AND BRAINS ON OPERATION LUNA MINOR, BUT THERE WAS STILL WORK FOR THE OTHER THUNDERBIRDS...
THE MAIN JOB WILL BE OUT IN SPACE, BOYS, BUT YOU'LL GIVE WHAT HELP YOU CAN ON EARTH, WHEREVER IT IS NEEDED.
CHECK, DAD.
WE'RE ON OUR WAY!
JOHN COOPER
THUNDERBIRD 1 AND THUNDERBIRD 2 TOOK OFF INTO THE DAWN LIGHT OVER TRACY ISLAND . . .
I'LL HAVE A QUICK SNOOP ROUND FOR THE NEAREST DISASTER SPOT, VIRGIL.
ROGER, SCOTT, BUT WHATEVER WE DO WILL ONLY BE A DROP IN THE OCEAN.
SHORTLY THUNDERBIRD 3 WITH ITS CREW OF THREE, BLASTED OFF INTO UNKNOWN HAZARDS, TO PERFORM A SEEMINGLY IMPOSSIBLE TASK . . .
JOB FOR TODAY... TO SHIFT A NEW-BORN MOON OR DESTROY IT. IT'S CRAZY, MAN.
THE MIGHTY ROCKET SHIP HURTLED ACROSS THE EARTH'S CURVATURE, AND ITS CREW GOT AWE-INSPIRING VISUALS . . .
GREAT GUNS, THE MAP'S BEEN ALTERED. FLORIDA'S BEEN SWAMPED. IT'S VANISHED.
FLORIDA GONE... WITH ALL ITS SPACE SHIP AND ROCKET COMPLEXES. WE'RE ON OUR OWN, FELLERS.
IT IS A...UM... HUMBLING THOUGHT THAT WITH ALL OUR SCIENTIFIC RESOURCES, WE ARE STILL AT THE MERCY OF NATURAL FORCES.
AND AS THUNDERBIRDS WERE GO, JEFF TRACY SAT ALONE . . .
GOOD LUCK, BOYS. THIS IS YOUR MOST DANGEROUS TASK... BUT THE FUTURE OF THE WORLD DEPENDS ON THUNDERBIRD 3.

Part 3 - dateline 07 March 2070

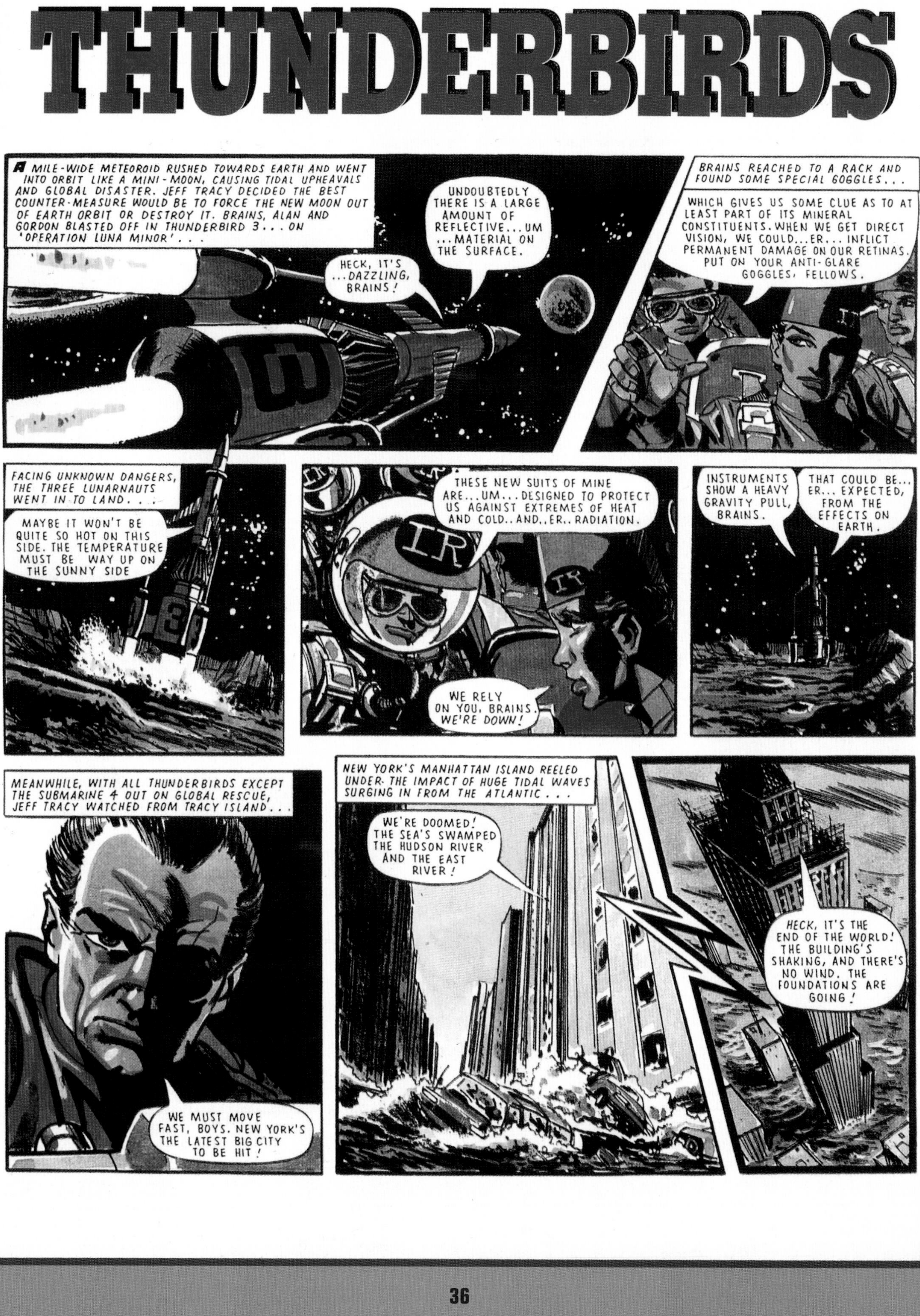
THUNDERBIRDS
A MILE-WIDE METEOROID RUSHED TOWARDS EARTH AND WENT INTO ORBIT LIKE A MINI-MOON, CAUSING TIDAL UPHEAVALS AND GLOBAL DISASTER. JEFF TRACY DECIDED THE BEST COUNTER-MEASURE WOULD BE TO FORCE THE NEW MOON OUT OF EARTH ORBIT OR DESTROY IT. BRAINS, ALAN AND GORDON BLASTED OFF IN THUNDERBIRD 3... ON 'OPERATION LUNA MINOR'...
HECK, IT'S ...DAZZLING, BRAINS!
UNDOUBTEDLY THERE IS A LARGE AMOUNT OF REFLECTIVE... UM ...MATERIAL ON THE SURFACE.
BRAINS REACHED TO A RACK AND FOUND SOME SPECIAL GOGGLES...
WHICH GIVES US SOME CLUE AS TO AT LEAST PART OF ITS MINERAL CONSTITUENTS. WHEN WE GET DIRECT VISION, WE COULD...ER... INFLICT PERMANENT DAMAGE ON OUR RETINAS. PUT ON YOUR ANTI-GLARE GOGGLES, FELLOWS.
FACING UNKNOWN DANGERS, THE THREE LUNARNAUTS WENT IN TO LAND...
MAYBE IT WON'T BE QUITE SO HOT ON THIS SIDE. THE TEMPERATURE MUST BE WAY UP ON THE SUNNY SIDE
THESE NEW SUITS OF MINE ARE...UM...DESIGNED TO PROTECT US AGAINST EXTREMES OF HEAT AND COLD.. AND.. ER.. RADIATION.
WE RELY ON YOU, BRAINS. WE'RE DOWN!
INSTRUMENTS SHOW A HEAVY GRAVITY PULL, BRAINS.
THAT COULD BE... ER... EXPECTED, FROM THE EFFECTS ON EARTH.
MEANWHILE, WITH ALL THUNDERBIRDS EXCEPT THE SUBMARINE 4 OUT ON GLOBAL RESCUE, JEFF TRACY WATCHED FROM TRACY ISLAND...
WE MUST MOVE FAST, BOYS. NEW YORK'S THE LATEST BIG CITY TO BE HIT!
NEW YORK'S MANHATTAN ISLAND REELED UNDER THE IMPACT OF HUGE TIDAL WAVES SURGING IN FROM THE ATLANTIC...
WE'RE DOOMED! THE SEA'S SWAMPED THE HUDSON RIVER AND THE EAST RIVER!
HECK, IT'S THE END OF THE WORLD! THE BUILDING'S SHAKING, AND THERE'S NO WIND. THE FOUNDATIONS ARE GOING!

Artist: John Cooper

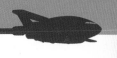

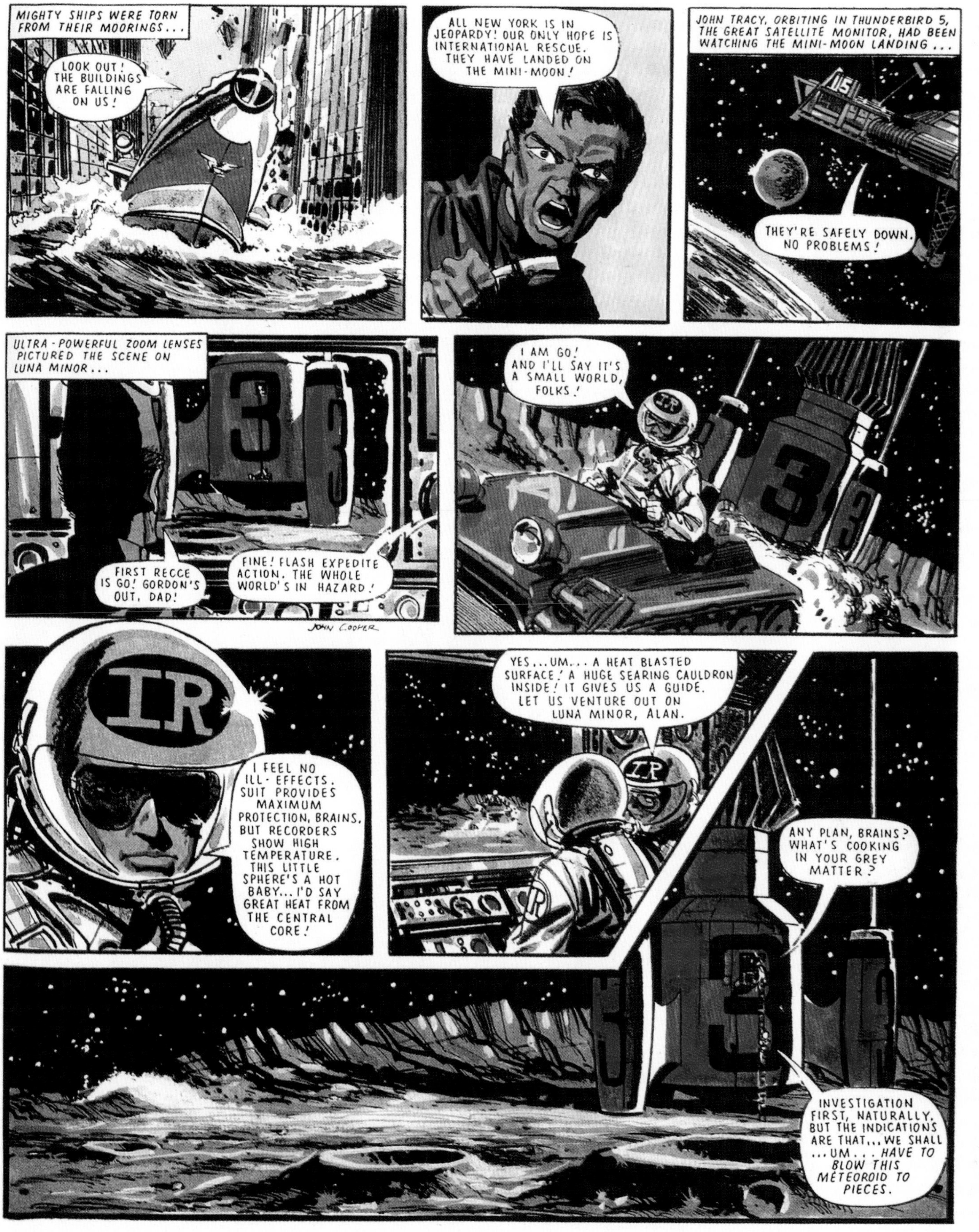
MIGHTY SHIPS WERE TORN FROM THEIR MOORINGS...
LOOK OUT! THE BUILDINGS ARE FALLING ON US!
ALL NEW YORK IS IN JEOPARDY! OUR ONLY HOPE IS INTERNATIONAL RESCUE. THEY HAVE LANDED ON THE MINI-MOON!
JOHN TRACY, ORBITING IN THUNDERBIRD 5, THE GREAT SATELLITE MONITOR, HAD BEEN WATCHING THE MINI-MOON LANDING...
THEY'RE SAFELY DOWN. NO PROBLEMS!
ULTRA-POWERFUL ZOOM LENSES PICTURED THE SCENE ON LUNA MINOR...
FIRST RECCE IS GO! GORDON'S OUT, DAD!
FINE! FLASH EXPEDITE ACTION. THE WHOLE WORLD'S IN HAZARD!
JOHN COOPER
I AM GO! AND I'LL SAY IT'S A SMALL WORLD, FOLKS!
I FEEL NO ILL-EFFECTS. SUIT PROVIDES MAXIMUM PROTECTION, BRAINS, BUT RECORDERS SHOW HIGH TEMPERATURE. THIS LITTLE SPHERE'S A HOT BABY... I'D SAY GREAT HEAT FROM THE CENTRAL CORE!
YES...UM... A HEAT BLASTED SURFACE! A HUGE SEARING CAULDRON INSIDE! IT GIVES US A GUIDE. LET US VENTURE OUT ON LUNA MINOR, ALAN.
ANY PLAN, BRAINS? WHAT'S COOKING IN YOUR GREY MATTER?
INVESTIGATION FIRST, NATURALLY. BUT THE INDICATIONS ARE THAT... WE SHALL ...UM... HAVE TO BLOW THIS METEOROID TO PIECES.

Part 4 - dateline 14 March 2070

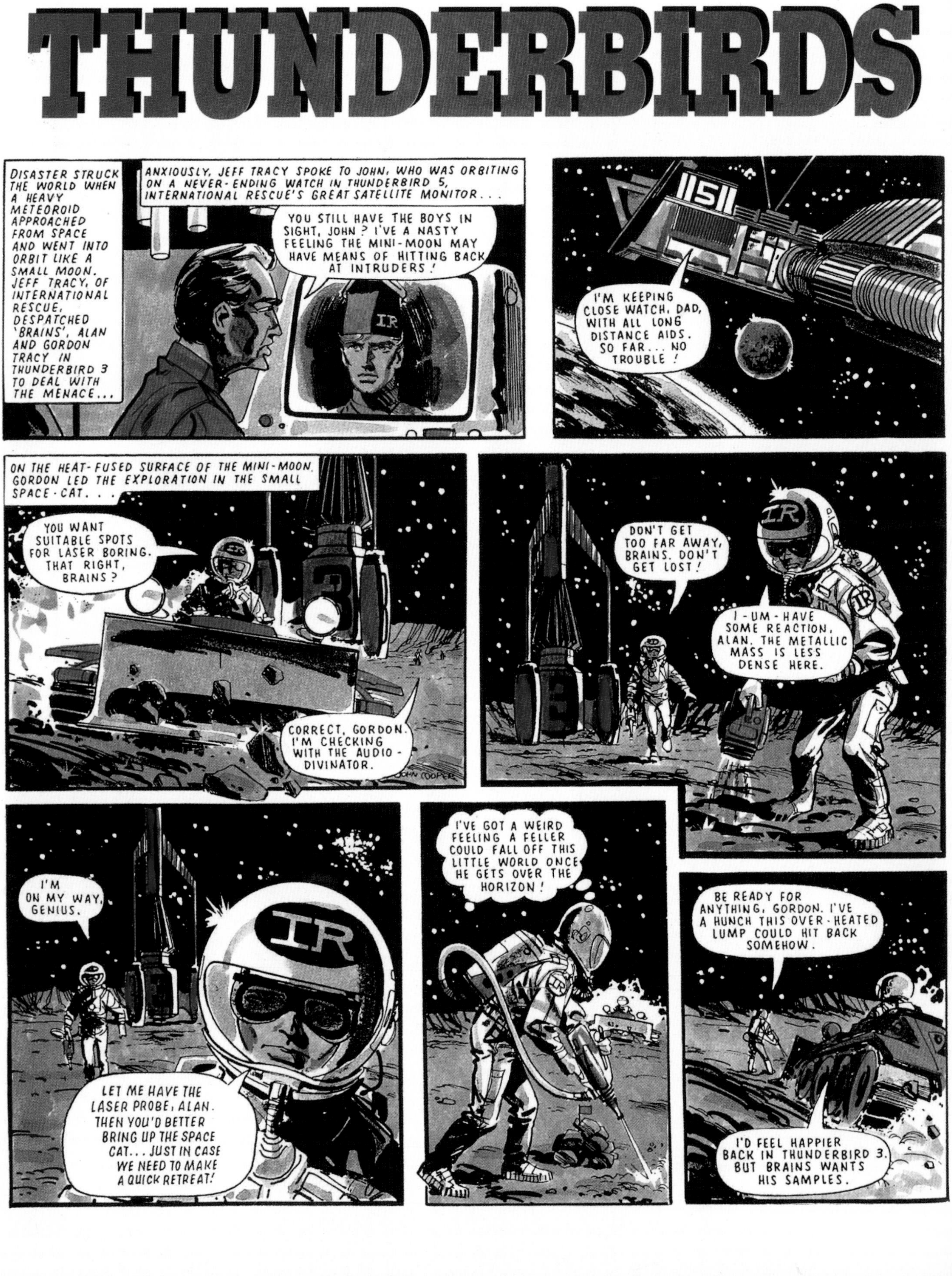
THUNDERBIRDS
DISASTER STRUCK THE WORLD WHEN A HEAVY METEOROID APPROACHED FROM SPACE AND WENT INTO ORBIT LIKE A SMALL MOON. JEFF TRACY, OF INTERNATIONAL RESCUE, DESPATCHED 'BRAINS', ALAN AND GORDON TRACY IN THUNDERBIRD 3 TO DEAL WITH THE MENACE...
ANXIOUSLY, JEFF TRACY SPOKE TO JOHN, WHO WAS ORBITING ON A NEVER-ENDING WATCH IN THUNDERBIRD 5, INTERNATIONAL RESCUE'S GREAT SATELLITE MONITOR...
YOU STILL HAVE THE BOYS IN SIGHT, JOHN? I'VE A NASTY FEELING THE MINI-MOON MAY HAVE MEANS OF HITTING BACK AT INTRUDERS!
I'M KEEPING CLOSE WATCH, DAD, WITH ALL LONG DISTANCE AIDS. SO FAR... NO TROUBLE!
ON THE HEAT-FUSED SURFACE OF THE MINI-MOON, GORDON LED THE EXPLORATION IN THE SMALL SPACE-CAT...
YOU WANT SUITABLE SPOTS FOR LASER BORING. THAT RIGHT, BRAINS?
CORRECT, GORDON. I'M CHECKING WITH THE AUDIO-DIVINATOR.
JOHN COOPER
DON'T GET TOO FAR AWAY, BRAINS. DON'T GET LOST!
I-UM-HAVE SOME REACTION, ALAN. THE METALLIC MASS IS LESS DENSE HERE.
I'M ON MY WAY, GENIUS.
LET ME HAVE THE LASER PROBE, ALAN. THEN YOU'D BETTER BRING UP THE SPACE CAT... JUST IN CASE WE NEED TO MAKE A QUICK RETREAT!
I'VE GOT A WEIRD FEELING A FELLER COULD FALL OFF THIS LITTLE WORLD ONCE HE GETS OVER THE HORIZON!
BE READY FOR ANYTHING, GORDON. I'VE A HUNCH THIS OVER-HEATED LUMP COULD HIT BACK SOMEHOW.
I'D FEEL HAPPIER BACK IN THUNDERBIRD 3. BUT BRAINS WANTS HIS SAMPLES.

Artist: John Cooper

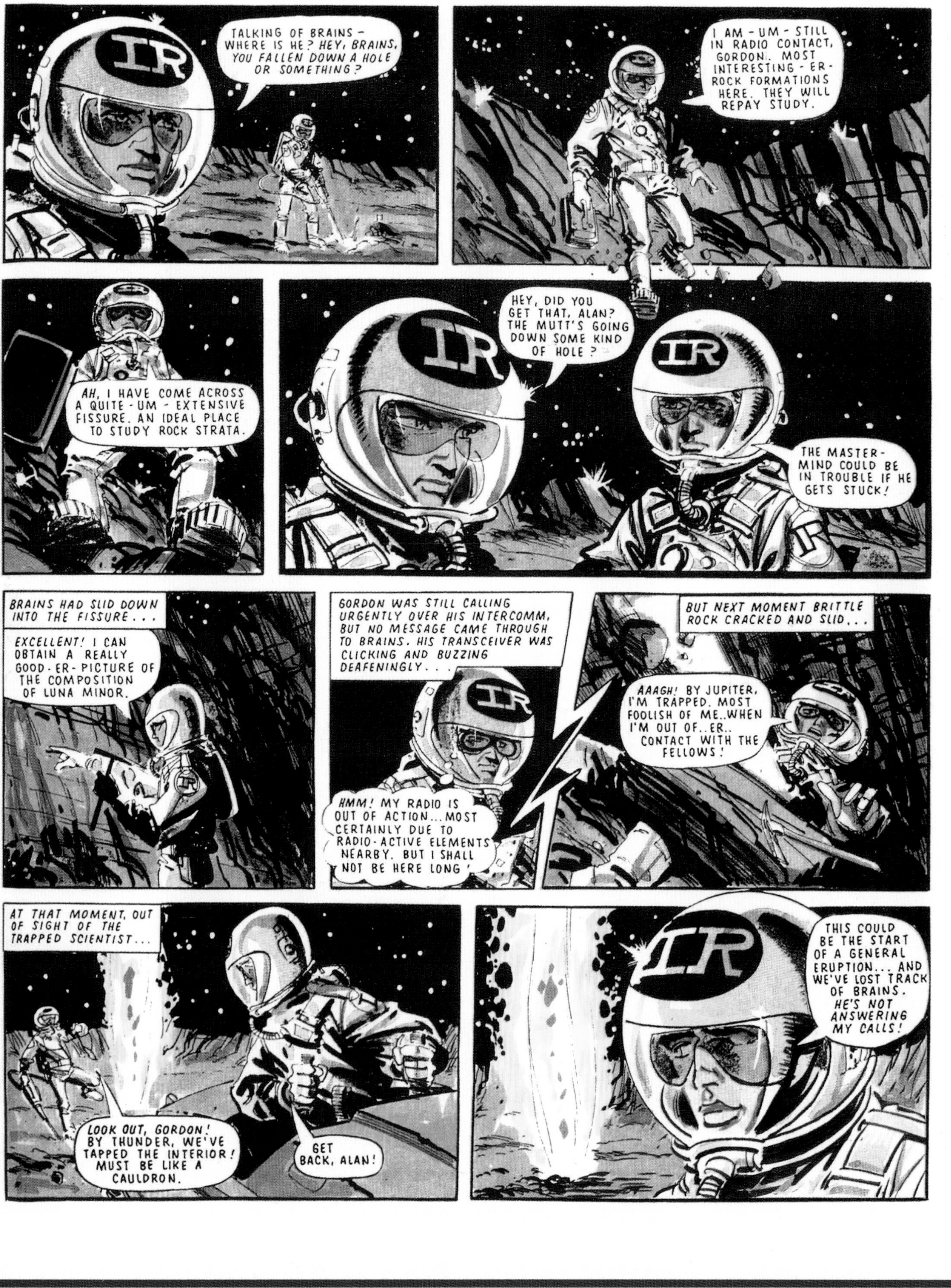

TALKING OF BRAINS - WHERE IS HE? HEY, BRAINS, YOU FALLEN DOWN A HOLE OR SOMETHING?
I AM - UM - STILL IN RADIO CONTACT, GORDON. MOST INTERESTING - ER - ROCK FORMATIONS HERE. THEY WILL REPAY STUDY.
AH, I HAVE COME ACROSS A QUITE - UM - EXTENSIVE FISSURE. AN IDEAL PLACE TO STUDY ROCK STRATA.
HEY, DID YOU GET THAT, ALAN? THE MUTT'S GOING DOWN SOME KIND OF HOLE?
THE MASTER-MIND COULD BE IN TROUBLE IF HE GETS STUCK!
BRAINS HAD SLID DOWN INTO THE FISSURE...
EXCELLENT! I CAN OBTAIN A REALLY GOOD-ER-PICTURE OF THE COMPOSITION OF LUNA MINOR.
GORDON WAS STILL CALLING URGENTLY OVER HIS INTERCOMM, BUT NO MESSAGE CAME THROUGH TO BRAINS. HIS TRANSCEIVER WAS CLICKING AND BUZZING DEAFENINGLY...
HMM! MY RADIO IS OUT OF ACTION... MOST CERTAINLY DUE TO RADIO-ACTIVE ELEMENTS NEARBY. BUT I SHALL NOT BE HERE LONG!
BUT NEXT MOMENT BRITTLE ROCK CRACKED AND SLID...
AAAGH! BY JUPITER, I'M TRAPPED. MOST FOOLISH OF ME..WHEN I'M OUT OF..ER.. CONTACT WITH THE FELLOWS!
AT THAT MOMENT, OUT OF SIGHT OF THE TRAPPED SCIENTIST...
LOOK OUT, GORDON! BY THUNDER, WE'VE TAPPED THE INTERIOR! MUST BE LIKE A CAULDRON.
GET BACK, ALAN!
THIS COULD BE THE START OF A GENERAL ERUPTION... AND WE'VE LOST TRACK OF BRAINS. HE'S NOT ANSWERING MY CALLS!

THUNDERBIRDS

Part 5 - dateline 21 March 2070

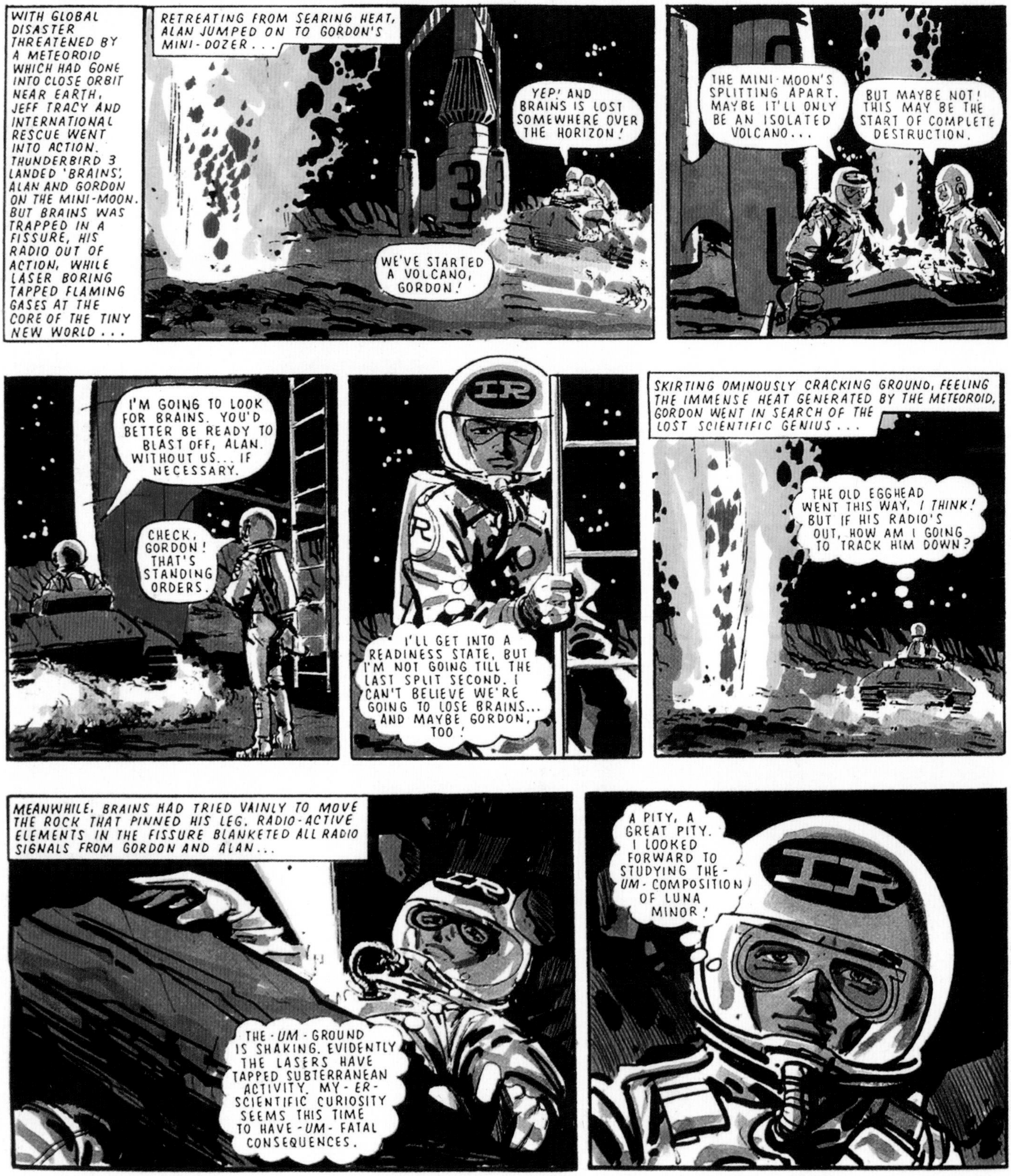
WITH GLOBAL DISASTER THREATENED BY A METEOROID WHICH HAD GONE INTO CLOSE ORBIT NEAR EARTH, JEFF TRACY AND INTERNATIONAL RESCUE WENT INTO ACTION. THUNDERBIRD 3 LANDED 'BRAINS', ALAN AND GORDON ON THE MINI-MOON. BUT BRAINS WAS TRAPPED IN A FISSURE, HIS RADIO OUT OF ACTION, WHILE LASER BORING TAPPED FLAMING GASES AT THE CORE OF THE TINY NEW WORLD . . .
RETREATING FROM SEARING HEAT, ALAN JUMPED ON TO GORDON'S MINI-DOZER . . .
WE'VE STARTED A VOLCANO, GORDON!
YEP! AND BRAINS IS LOST SOMEWHERE OVER THE HORIZON!
3
THE MINI-MOON'S SPLITTING APART. MAYBE IT'LL ONLY BE AN ISOLATED VOLCANO...
BUT MAYBE NOT! THIS MAY BE THE START OF COMPLETE DESTRUCTION.
I'M GOING TO LOOK FOR BRAINS. YOU'D BETTER BE READY TO BLAST OFF, ALAN. WITHOUT US... IF NECESSARY.
CHECK, GORDON! THAT'S STANDING ORDERS.
IR
I'LL GET INTO A READINESS STATE, BUT I'M NOT GOING TILL THE LAST SPLIT SECOND. I CAN'T BELIEVE WE'RE GOING TO LOSE BRAINS... AND MAYBE GORDON, TOO!
SKIRTING OMINOUSLY CRACKING GROUND, FEELING THE IMMENSE HEAT GENERATED BY THE METEOROID, GORDON WENT IN SEARCH OF THE LOST SCIENTIFIC GENIUS . . .
THE OLD EGGHEAD WENT THIS WAY, I THINK! BUT IF HIS RADIO'S OUT, HOW AM I GOING TO TRACK HIM DOWN?
MEANWHILE, BRAINS HAD TRIED VAINLY TO MOVE THE ROCK THAT PINNED HIS LEG. RADIO-ACTIVE ELEMENTS IN THE FISSURE BLANKETED ALL RADIO SIGNALS FROM GORDON AND ALAN...
IR
THE-UM-GROUND IS SHAKING. EVIDENTLY THE LASERS HAVE TAPPED SUBTERRANEAN ACTIVITY. MY-ER-SCIENTIFIC CURIOSITY SEEMS THIS TIME TO HAVE-UM-FATAL CONSEQUENCES.
A PITY, A GREAT PITY. I LOOKED FORWARD TO STUDYING THE-UM-COMPOSITION OF LUNA MINOR!
IR

Artist: John Cooper

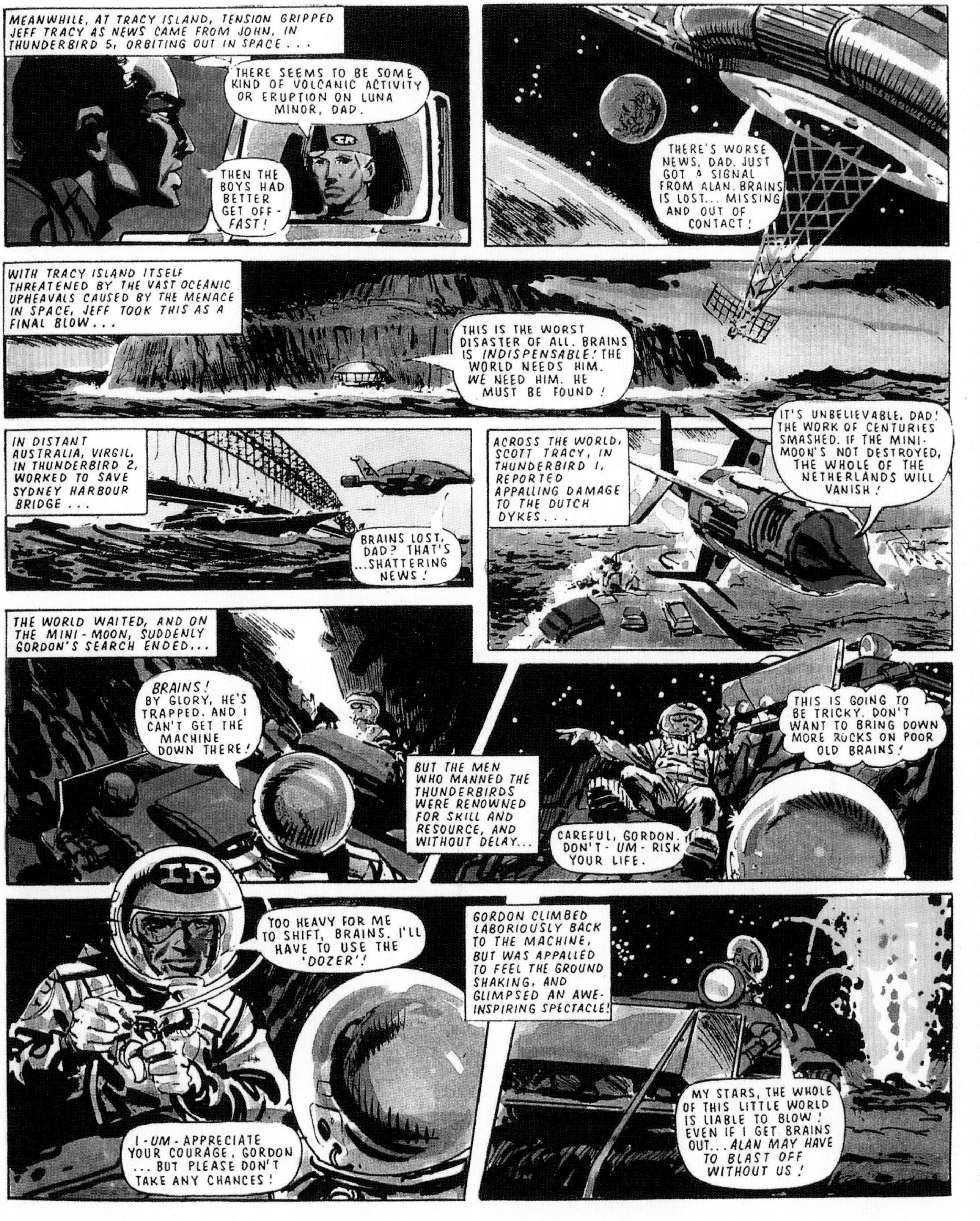
MEANWHILE, AT TRACY ISLAND, TENSION GRIPPED JEFF TRACY AS NEWS CAME FROM JOHN, IN THUNDERBIRD 5, ORBITING OUT IN SPACE . . .
THERE SEEMS TO BE SOME KIND OF VOLCANIC ACTIVITY OR ERUPTION ON LUNA MINOR, DAD.
THEN THE BOYS HAD BETTER GET OFF - FAST!
THERE'S WORSE NEWS, DAD. JUST GOT A SIGNAL FROM ALAN. BRAINS IS LOST... MISSING AND OUT OF CONTACT!
WITH TRACY ISLAND ITSELF THREATENED BY THE VAST OCEANIC UPHEAVALS CAUSED BY THE MENACE IN SPACE, JEFF TOOK THIS AS A FINAL BLOW . . .
THIS IS THE WORST DISASTER OF ALL. BRAINS IS INDISPENSABLE! THE WORLD NEEDS HIM. WE NEED HIM. HE MUST BE FOUND!
IN DISTANT AUSTRALIA, VIRGIL, IN THUNDERBIRD 2, WORKED TO SAVE SYDNEY HARBOUR BRIDGE . . .
BRAINS LOST, DAD? THAT'S ...SHATTERING NEWS!
ACROSS THE WORLD, SCOTT TRACY, IN THUNDERBIRD 1, REPORTED APPALLING DAMAGE TO THE DUTCH DYKES . . .
IT'S UNBELIEVABLE, DAD! THE WORK OF CENTURIES SMASHED. IF THE MINI-MOON'S NOT DESTROYED, THE WHOLE OF THE NETHERLANDS WILL VANISH!
THE WORLD WAITED, AND ON THE MINI-MOON, SUDDENLY GORDON'S SEARCH ENDED...
BRAINS! BY GLORY, HE'S TRAPPED. AND I CAN'T GET THE MACHINE DOWN THERE!
BUT THE MEN WHO MANNED THE THUNDERBIRDS WERE RENOWNED FOR SKILL AND RESOURCE, AND WITHOUT DELAY...
THIS IS GOING TO BE TRICKY. DON'T WANT TO BRING DOWN MORE ROCKS ON POOR OLD BRAINS!
CAREFUL, GORDON. DON'T - UM - RISK YOUR LIFE.
TOO HEAVY FOR ME TO SHIFT, BRAINS. I'LL HAVE TO USE THE 'DOZER'!
I - UM - APPRECIATE YOUR COURAGE, GORDON ... BUT PLEASE DON'T TAKE ANY CHANCES!
GORDON CLIMBED LABORIOUSLY BACK TO THE MACHINE, BUT WAS APPALLED TO FEEL THE GROUND SHAKING, AND GLIMPSED AN AWE-INSPIRING SPECTACLE!
MY STARS, THE WHOLE OF THIS LITTLE WORLD IS LIABLE TO BLOW! EVEN IF I GET BRAINS OUT... ALAN MAY HAVE TO BLAST OFF WITHOUT US!

Part 6 - dateline 28 March 2070

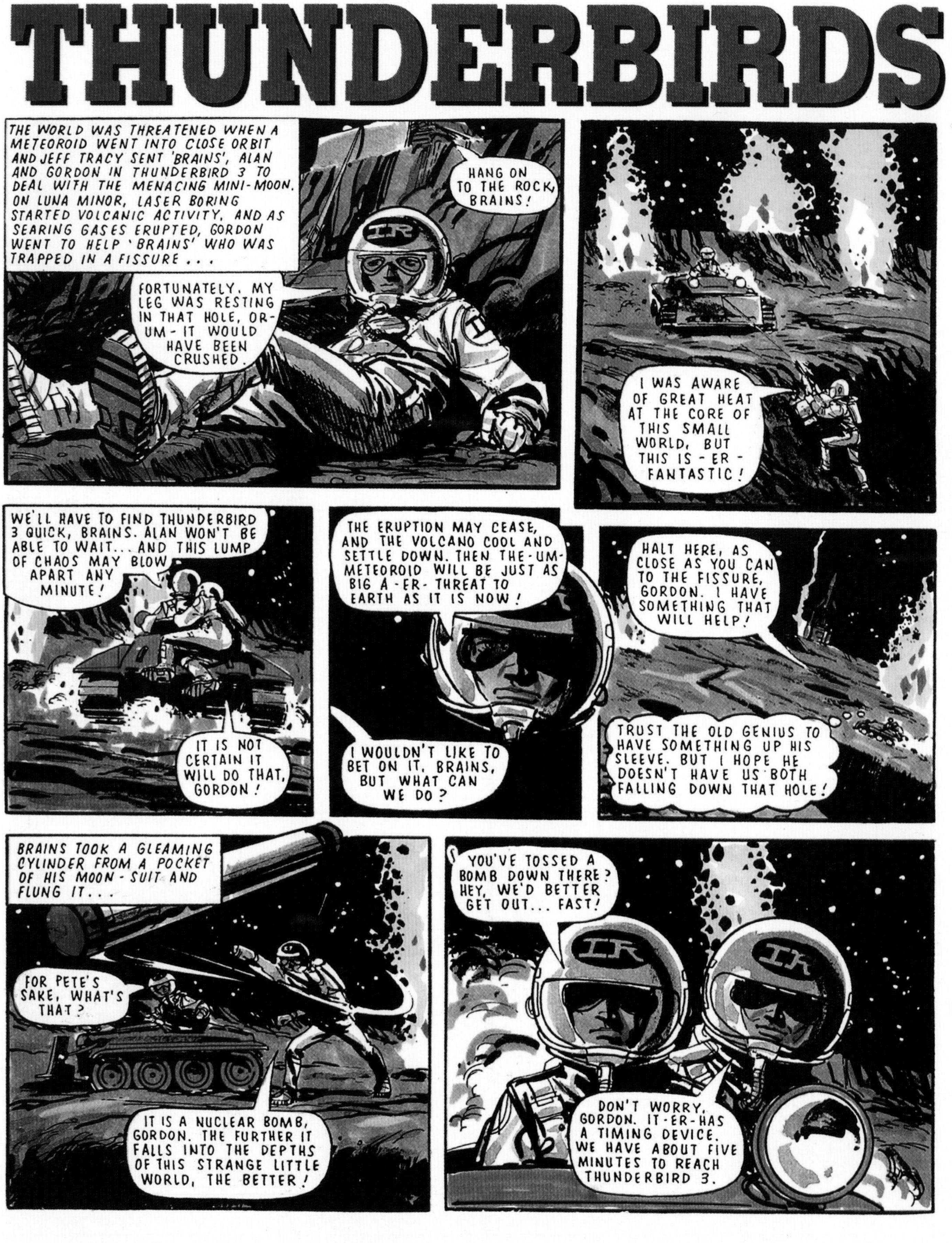
THUNDERBIRDS
THE WORLD WAS THREATENED WHEN A METEOROID WENT INTO CLOSE ORBIT AND JEFF TRACY SENT 'BRAINS', ALAN AND GORDON IN THUNDERBIRD 3 TO DEAL WITH THE MENACING MINI-MOON. ON LUNA MINOR, LASER BORING STARTED VOLCANIC ACTIVITY, AND AS SEARING GASES ERUPTED, GORDON WENT TO HELP 'BRAINS' WHO WAS TRAPPED IN A FISSURE . . .
HANG ON TO THE ROCK, BRAINS!
FORTUNATELY, MY LEG WAS RESTING IN THAT HOLE, OR-UM-IT WOULD HAVE BEEN CRUSHED.
I WAS AWARE OF GREAT HEAT AT THE CORE OF THIS SMALL WORLD, BUT THIS IS-ER-FANTASTIC!
WE'LL HAVE TO FIND THUNDERBIRD 3 QUICK, BRAINS. ALAN WON'T BE ABLE TO WAIT... AND THIS LUMP OF CHAOS MAY BLOW APART ANY MINUTE!
IT IS NOT CERTAIN IT WILL DO THAT, GORDON!
THE ERUPTION MAY CEASE, AND THE VOLCANO COOL AND SETTLE DOWN. THEN THE-UM-METEOROID WILL BE JUST AS BIG A-ER-THREAT TO EARTH AS IT IS NOW!
I WOULDN'T LIKE TO BET ON IT, BRAINS, BUT WHAT CAN WE DO?
HALT HERE, AS CLOSE AS YOU CAN TO THE FISSURE, GORDON. I HAVE SOMETHING THAT WILL HELP!
TRUST THE OLD GENIUS TO HAVE SOMETHING UP HIS SLEEVE. BUT I HOPE HE DOESN'T HAVE US BOTH FALLING DOWN THAT HOLE!
BRAINS TOOK A GLEAMING CYLINDER FROM A POCKET OF HIS MOON-SUIT AND FLUNG IT...
FOR PETE'S SAKE, WHAT'S THAT?
IT IS A NUCLEAR BOMB, GORDON. THE FURTHER IT FALLS INTO THE DEPTHS OF THIS STRANGE LITTLE WORLD, THE BETTER!
YOU'VE TOSSED A BOMB DOWN THERE? HEY, WE'D BETTER GET OUT... FAST!
DON'T WORRY, GORDON. IT-ER-HAS A TIMING DEVICE. WE HAVE ABOUT FIVE MINUTES TO REACH THUNDERBIRD 3.

Artist: John Cooper

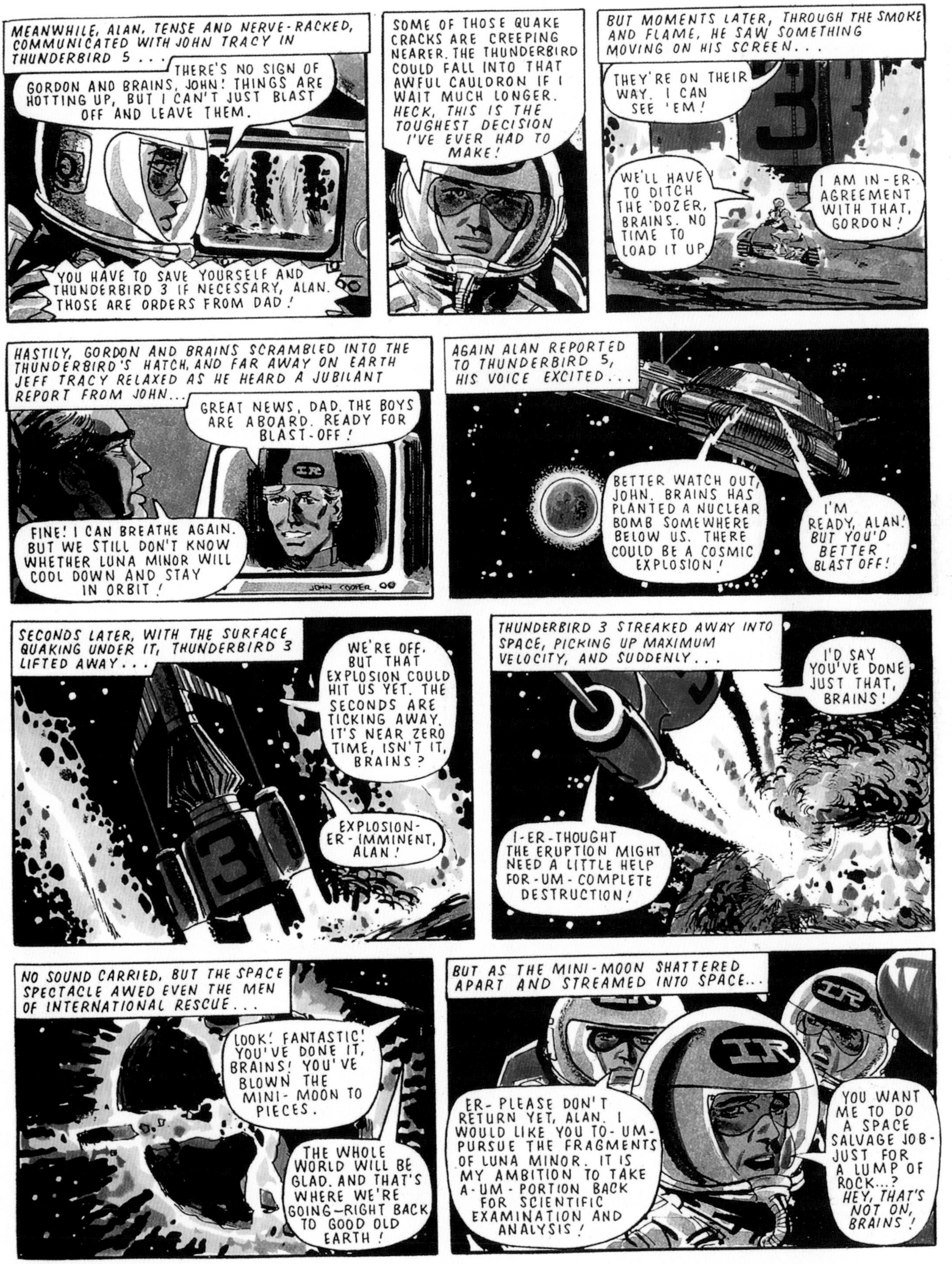
MEANWHILE, ALAN, TENSE AND NERVE-RACKED, COMMUNICATED WITH JOHN TRACY IN THUNDERBIRD 5 . . .
THERE'S NO SIGN OF GORDON AND BRAINS, JOHN! THINGS ARE HOTTING UP, BUT I CAN'T JUST BLAST OFF AND LEAVE THEM.
YOU HAVE TO SAVE YOURSELF AND THUNDERBIRD 3 IF NECESSARY, ALAN. THOSE ARE ORDERS FROM DAD!
SOME OF THOSE QUAKE CRACKS ARE CREEPING NEARER. THE THUNDERBIRD COULD FALL INTO THAT AWFUL CAULDRON IF I WAIT MUCH LONGER. HECK, THIS IS THE TOUGHEST DECISION I'VE EVER HAD TO MAKE!
BUT MOMENTS LATER, THROUGH THE SMOKE AND FLAME, HE SAW SOMETHING MOVING ON HIS SCREEN . . .
THEY'RE ON THEIR WAY. I CAN SEE 'EM!
WE'LL HAVE TO DITCH THE 'DOZER, BRAINS. NO TIME TO LOAD IT UP.
I AM IN-ER-AGREEMENT WITH THAT, GORDON!
HASTILY, GORDON AND BRAINS SCRAMBLED INTO THE THUNDERBIRD'S HATCH, AND FAR AWAY ON EARTH JEFF TRACY RELAXED AS HE HEARD A JUBILANT REPORT FROM JOHN . . .
GREAT NEWS, DAD. THE BOYS ARE ABOARD. READY FOR BLAST-OFF!
FINE! I CAN BREATHE AGAIN. BUT WE STILL DON'T KNOW WHETHER LUNA MINOR WILL COOL DOWN AND STAY IN ORBIT!
JOHN COOPER
AGAIN ALAN REPORTED TO THUNDERBIRD 5, HIS VOICE EXCITED . . .
BETTER WATCH OUT, JOHN. BRAINS HAS PLANTED A NUCLEAR BOMB SOMEWHERE BELOW US. THERE COULD BE A COSMIC EXPLOSION!
I'M READY, ALAN! BUT YOU'D BETTER BLAST OFF!
SECONDS LATER, WITH THE SURFACE QUAKING UNDER IT, THUNDERBIRD 3 LIFTED AWAY . . .
WE'RE OFF. BUT THAT EXPLOSION COULD HIT US YET. THE SECONDS ARE TICKING AWAY. IT'S NEAR ZERO TIME, ISN'T IT, BRAINS?
EXPLOSION-ER-IMMINENT, ALAN!
THUNDERBIRD 3 STREAKED AWAY INTO SPACE, PICKING UP MAXIMUM VELOCITY, AND SUDDENLY . . .
I'D SAY YOU'VE DONE JUST THAT, BRAINS!
I-ER-THOUGHT THE ERUPTION MIGHT NEED A LITTLE HELP FOR-UM-COMPLETE DESTRUCTION!
NO SOUND CARRIED, BUT THE SPACE SPECTACLE AWED EVEN THE MEN OF INTERNATIONAL RESCUE . . .
LOOK! FANTASTIC! YOU'VE DONE IT, BRAINS! YOU'VE BLOWN THE MINI-MOON TO PIECES.
THE WHOLE WORLD WILL BE GLAD. AND THAT'S WHERE WE'RE GOING—RIGHT BACK TO GOOD OLD EARTH!
BUT AS THE MINI-MOON SHATTERED APART AND STREAMED INTO SPACE . . .
ER-PLEASE DON'T RETURN YET, ALAN. I WOULD LIKE YOU TO-UM-PURSUE THE FRAGMENTS OF LUNA MINOR. IT IS MY AMBITION TO TAKE A-UM-PORTION BACK FOR SCIENTIFIC EXAMINATION AND ANALYSIS!
YOU WANT ME TO DO A SPACE SALVAGE JOB-JUST FOR A LUMP OF ROCK...? HEY, THAT'S NOT ON, BRAINS!

Part 7 - dateline 04 April 2070

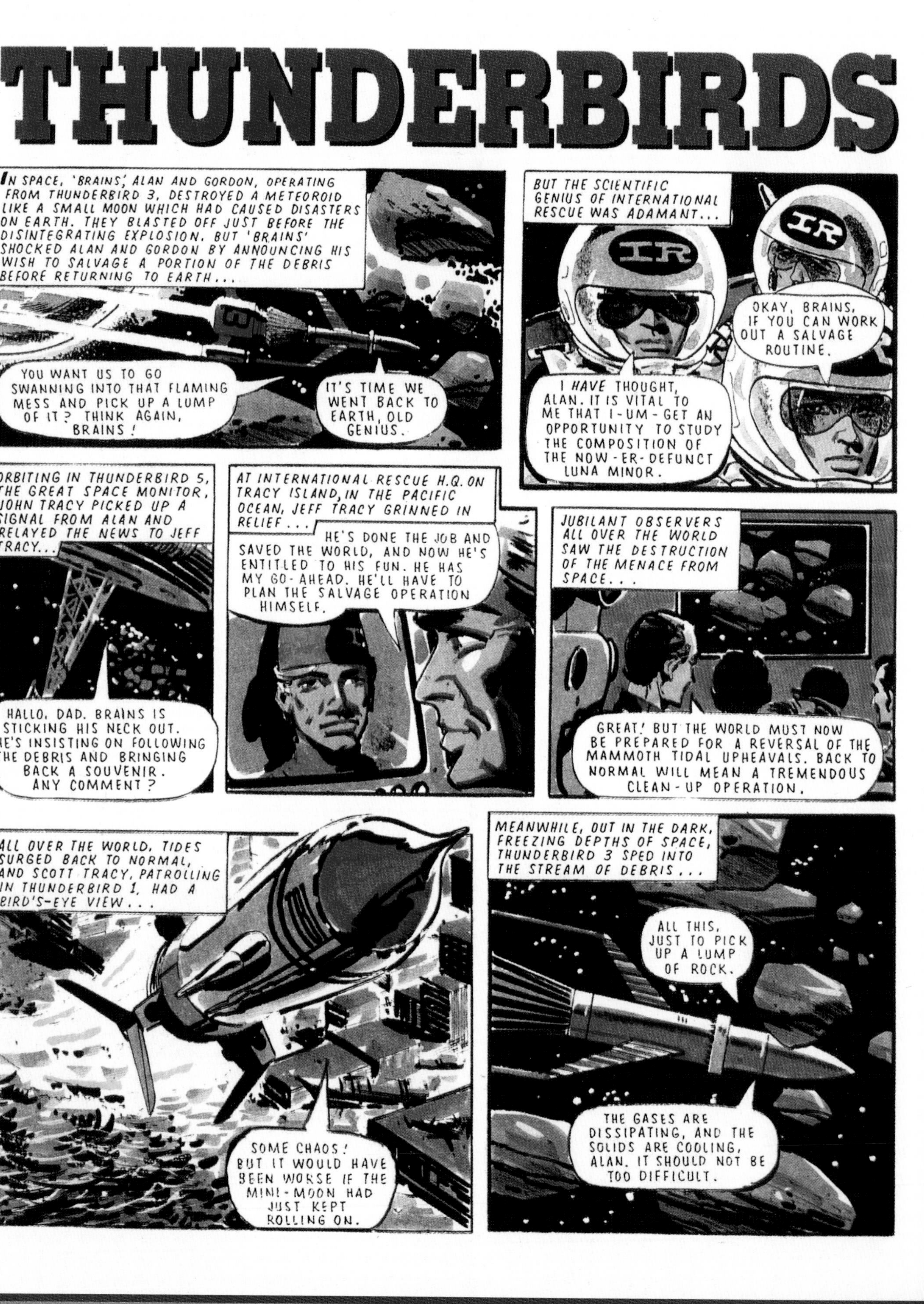
THUNDERBIRDS
IN SPACE, 'BRAINS,' ALAN AND GORDON, OPERATING FROM THUNDERBIRD 3, DESTROYED A METEOROID LIKE A SMALL MOON WHICH HAD CAUSED DISASTERS ON EARTH. THEY BLASTED OFF JUST BEFORE THE DISINTEGRATING EXPLOSION. BUT 'BRAINS' SHOCKED ALAN AND GORDON BY ANNOUNCING HIS WISH TO SALVAGE A PORTION OF THE DEBRIS BEFORE RETURNING TO EARTH...
YOU WANT US TO GO SWANNING INTO THAT FLAMING MESS AND PICK UP A LUMP OF IT? THINK AGAIN, BRAINS!
IT'S TIME WE WENT BACK TO EARTH, OLD GENIUS.
BUT THE SCIENTIFIC GENIUS OF INTERNATIONAL RESCUE WAS ADAMANT...
I HAVE THOUGHT, ALAN. IT IS VITAL TO ME THAT I-UM-GET AN OPPORTUNITY TO STUDY THE COMPOSITION OF THE NOW-ER-DEFUNCT LUNA MINOR.
OKAY, BRAINS, IF YOU CAN WORK OUT A SALVAGE ROUTINE.
ORBITING IN THUNDERBIRD 5, THE GREAT SPACE MONITOR, JOHN TRACY PICKED UP A SIGNAL FROM ALAN AND RELAYED THE NEWS TO JEFF TRACY...
HALLO, DAD. BRAINS IS STICKING HIS NECK OUT. HE'S INSISTING ON FOLLOWING THE DEBRIS AND BRINGING BACK A SOUVENIR. ANY COMMENT?
AT INTERNATIONAL RESCUE H.Q. ON TRACY ISLAND, IN THE PACIFIC OCEAN, JEFF TRACY GRINNED IN RELIEF...
HE'S DONE THE JOB AND SAVED THE WORLD, AND NOW HE'S ENTITLED TO HIS FUN. HE HAS MY GO-AHEAD. HE'LL HAVE TO PLAN THE SALVAGE OPERATION HIMSELF.
JUBILANT OBSERVERS ALL OVER THE WORLD SAW THE DESTRUCTION OF THE MENACE FROM SPACE...
GREAT! BUT THE WORLD MUST NOW BE PREPARED FOR A REVERSAL OF THE MAMMOTH TIDAL UPHEAVALS. BACK TO NORMAL WILL MEAN A TREMENDOUS CLEAN-UP OPERATION.
ALL OVER THE WORLD, TIDES SURGED BACK TO NORMAL, AND SCOTT TRACY, PATROLLING IN THUNDERBIRD 1, HAD A BIRD'S-EYE VIEW...
SOME CHAOS! BUT IT WOULD HAVE BEEN WORSE IF THE MINI-MOON HAD JUST KEPT ROLLING ON.
MEANWHILE, OUT IN THE DARK, FREEZING DEPTHS OF SPACE, THUNDERBIRD 3 SPED INTO THE STREAM OF DEBRIS...
ALL THIS, JUST TO PICK UP A LUMP OF ROCK.
THE GASES ARE DISSIPATING, AND THE SOLIDS ARE COOLING, ALAN. IT SHOULD NOT BE TOO DIFFICULT.

Artist: John Cooper

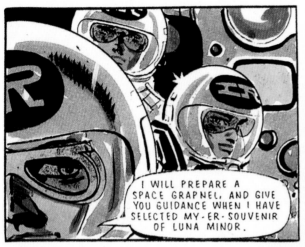

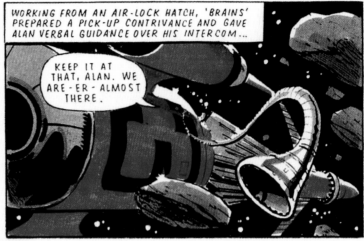

I WILL PREPARE A SPACE GRAPNEL, AND GIVE YOU GUIDANCE WHEN I HAVE SELECTED MY-ER-SOUVENIR OF LUNA MINOR.
WORKING FROM AN AIR-LOCK HATCH, 'BRAINS' PREPARED A PICK-UP CONTRIVANCE AND GAVE ALAN VERBAL GUIDANCE OVER HIS INTERCOM...
KEEP IT AT THAT, ALAN. WE ARE-ER-ALMOST THERE.
ALAN'S SUPERB SKILL BROUGHT PICK-UP AND ROCK SAMPLE CLOSER TOGETHER, AND SOON...
CONTACT HAS BEEN MADE, ALAN. WE ARE NOW-UM-HOME AND DRY.
JUST AS WELL, BRAINS. GORDON AND I ARE LOOKING FORWARD TO A REAL HOME-COOKED MEAL.
WITH THE ROCK SAFELY IN THE HATCH, THUNDERBIRD 3 PLUMMETED TOWARDS EARTH...
I BELIEVE MY RESEARCH WILL BE MOST INTERESTING. I SHALL START IMMEDIATELY.
I'M SURE IT WILL, GENIUS, BUT I'M GOING TO START RESEARCH ON A NICE THICK STEAK.
SAFELY BACK AT TRACY ISLAND, BRAINS REFUSED TO BE PARTED FROM HIS SOUVENIR
WANT ANY HELP, BRAINS?
NO, THANK YOU, MISTER TRACY. YOU MAY SEND IN A-UM-SNACK OR LIGHT MEAL. I SHALL BE BUSY FOR SOME TIME.
WHEN SCOTT AND VIRGIL RETURNED IN THUNDERBIRDS ONE AND TWO, HOURS LATER, BRAINS WAS STILL LOCKED IN HIS LABORATORY...
THE EMERGENCY IS OVER, AND THE WORLD IS NOW TAKING STOCK. ALL DECLARED DISASTER AREAS WILL RECEIVE IMMEDIATE HELP. THE WORLD THANKS INTERNATIONAL RESCUE.
GREAT. BUT IT'S BRAINS I'M WONDERING ABOUT.
THE TRACY FAMILY WAITED IMPATIENTLY, BUT STILL MANY HOURS PASSED BEFORE 'BRAINS' ALLOWED THEM INTO HIS LABORATORY, AND THEN...
GREAT GUNS, IT'S.. IT'S A DIAMOND!
YES, GENTLEMEN, A DIAMOND-FUSED AND COMPRESSED BY THE GREAT HEAT OF LUNA MINOR. POLISHED AND CUT BY...UM... MYSELF.
THIS MEANS THERE MIGHT BE HUNDREDS, PERHAPS THOUSANDS MORE PIECES LIKE THIS FLOATING ABOUT IN SPACE!
YES, GORDON... A FRUITFUL FIELD FOR DARING SPACE PROSPECTORS.
BRAINS, THIS IS WORTH A COLOSSAL FORTUNE. IT COULD FINANCE INTERNATIONAL RESCUE FOR YEARS TO COME.
BUT BRAINS SUDDENLY LOOKED STUBBORN...
NO, SCOTT, THIS IS A SCIENTIFIC SAMPLE, AND WILL REMAIN SO. BESIDES, THERE WOULD NOT BE ENOUGH..ER.. MONEY IN THE WORLD TO BUY A DIAMOND THIS SIZE...
... AND IT WOULD TAKE ME YEARS TO CUT IT INTO SMALLER GEMS. I AM-ER-MUCH TOO BUSY. IT WILL REMAIN WITH ME AS A REMINDER OF LUNA MINOR.

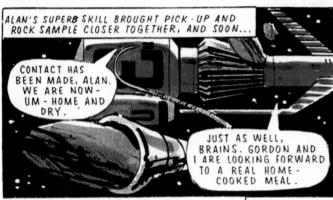

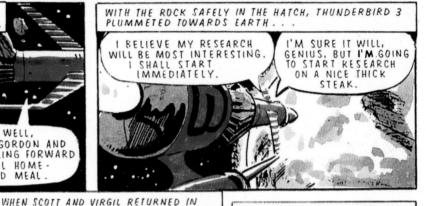

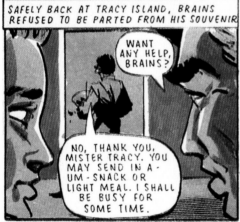

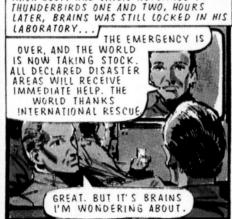

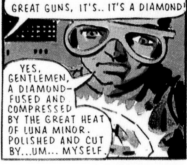

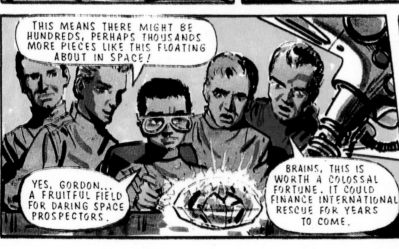

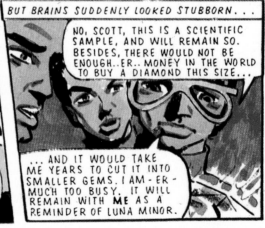

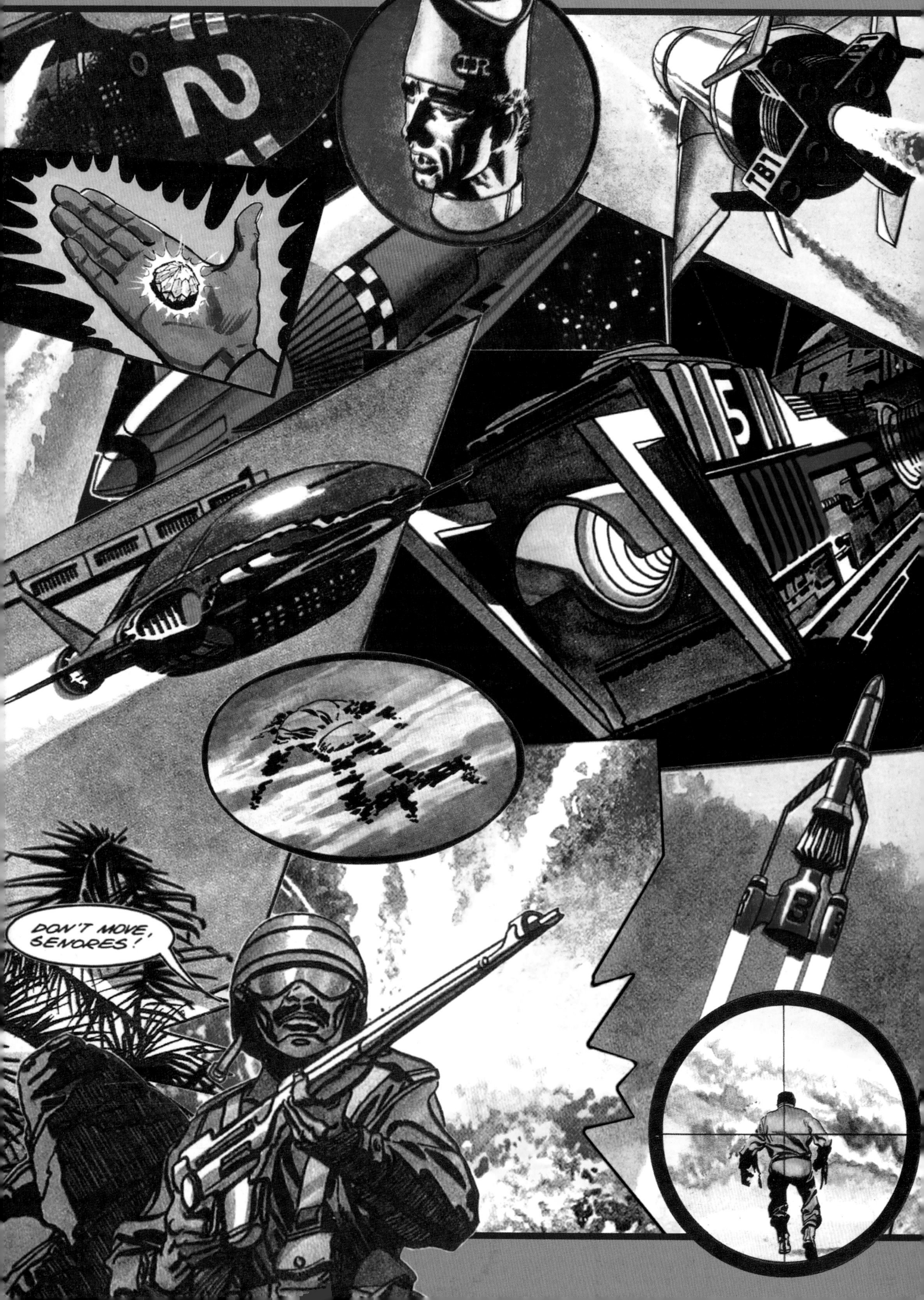
DON'T MOVE, SENORES!

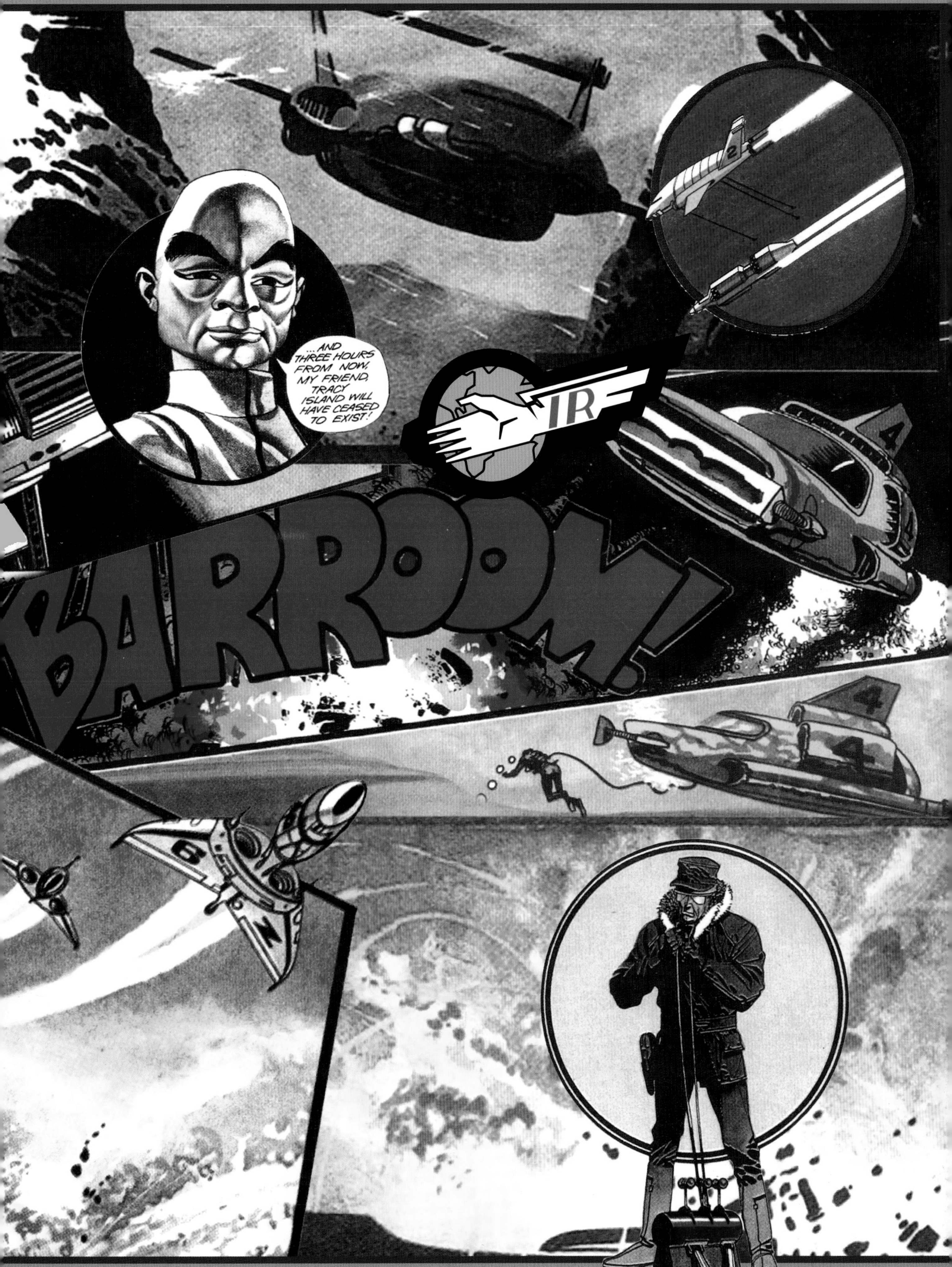

...AND THREE HOURS FROM NOW, MY FRIEND, TRACY ISLAND WILL HAVE CEASED TO EXIST!
IR
BARROOM!

FRANK BELLAMY
BUT THERE IS ONE ANSWER! THE CALL GOES OUT TO THUNDERBIRD FIVE, ORBITING THE EARTH ON CEASELESS WATCH!
5

CLASSIC COMICS
EGMONT